REAL WORLD INVESTING

A SENSIBLE APPROACH FROM THE GUY WITHOUT THE TIE

BY GARY SILVERMAN, CFP®

Real World Investing:
A Sensible Approach from the Guy Without the Tie

Author: Gary Silverman
Published by Austin Brothers Publishing

Fort Worth, Texas

www.abpbooks.com

ISBN 978-0-9845366-8-9

Austin Brothers
Publishing

Books are available in quantity for promotional or educational use. Contact Austin Brothers Publishing for information at 3616 Sutter Ct., Fort Worth, TX 76137 or wterrya@gmail.com.

This and other books published by Austin Brothers Publishing can be purchased at www.abpbooks.com.

Printed in the United States of America

2016 -- First Edition

This is where I'm supposed to thank everyone who is responsible for this book. The reality is that this is an impossible task since every person who has touched my life in some way influenced this book. With the limitation of my rather poor memory, let's get started.

To my parents, who through that nurturing process gave me the desire to read and learn; the teachers who provided room for question and debate; and to Alan who gave me the chance to grow and spread my wings in this crazy world of financial planning and investing.

To those who helped me grow my firm and then got back to their truer passions: Rene, Veronica, and Sarah; as well as those who are still on the journey with me: Michelle, DaNella, Kody, and Tina (who made sure that this book actually got finished); with a special shout-out to Mona who tried her best to make me grammatically correct...to varying levels of success.

To Nick, whom though we seldom talk love and safety always attends our discussions, with God hugging us both in the process.

And, never least, to my wife and love, Joanne. For some reason she's stuck with me through thick and thin (neither of which were particularly fun), my varying degrees of inattentiveness (squirrel!), and gave up part of our life together so this book could be.

Contents

PROLOGUE
Why This Book?

This book describes how I go about managing other people's money. While there is some *how to* inside, my goal is getting you to think about the investing process, not teach you the mechanics of how to invest. Whether you go on to manage a pension fund, your family's money, your own 401(k) account at work, or just want to know what's happening inside a mutual fund you happen to own, this book will help you make sense of it.

When I got my first full-time civilian job (I was in the Navy prior to that), I knew I should invest for the future. However, I didn't have a clue what investing was all about. So I began attending seminars to learn. I hired a person who called herself a financial planner after going to her seminar. Over the next several years, during an up market, she with her skills and expertise managed to lose half of my money. I decided that maybe I should learn a bit about investing myself.

Initially I figured that I'd learn how to research and decide which stock, bond, or other investment would go up the most in any particular year. I didn't realize that this was an impossible task and one that put me into direct competition with some of the brightest minds and largest companies in the world. Still I studied, earned an MBA, and became a Certified Financial Planner® professional.

As good a foundation as that was, it took time, experience, and a lot more study (that has not ended) for me to figure out the "secret" to investing. It's not really much of a secret. In fact, the only reason that most people don't do it is because it's just not sexy and doesn't promise quick riches. I began helping friends and family, eventually transitioning to a full-time investment manager. During the last twenty plus years I've guided my clients in preparing for their future.

While a main part of my business is managing investments for other people, some of you would rather do it yourself. Perhaps you don't trust financial professionals, maybe you just don't want to pay the money, or you might just find it interesting and fun... a hobby if you will. So I wanted to put together over three decades of knowledge I had about investing to help others who want to help themselves.

Once we gathered the material together, my in-house wordsmith, Tina, told me that we had about 1000 pages of material. And that was before I had a chance to flesh it out a bit. Investing is more than just the basic material. It's also how you have to change with the economy, technological advances, the issuance of new types of investment products, and the ever-changing tax laws. That takes a lot of words.

Then there is you. Your psychological makeup is as important (if not more important) a consideration on how you should invest, as is your age, income, and tax bracket. Each and every one of you has your own unique situation and look at the risks and rewards of investing differently.

Soon I realized that it was impossible for me to write a book that could teach someone how to invest in a way that would satisfy me. That's why I shifted instead to tell you how I do it for myself and my clients. It might not cover everything, but let's face it, no one wants to read a 1000 page book.

So for those of you looking for a book that tells you all the ins and outs of investing... well, this isn't it. But don't worry, because if you're looking for a way to invest wisely and not have to pay someone like me to do it for you, then the section on do-it-yourself investing (Chapters 9 and 10) was written for you. While it may not be perfect (nothing about investing is), following my recommendations will put you ahead of the vast majority of casual investors. Still, you'd do well by reading the rest of the book as well.

And though I've stated that this is a book about investing, I know that most of you have one primary investment goal: Retirement. So I've put in a chapter talking about getting ready for that.

Let's get started.

CHAPTER 1
The Road To Investing

There are stepping stones to investing. For instance, if you don't have a savings program for the things you know are going to happen, you will need to either rob from your investments or borrow the money. If you don't have an emergency fund for the things you weren't expecting, you will need to either rob from your investments or borrow the money. And if you have a sizeable amount of debt, then you will be constrained from being able to invest as you have interest and principle to pay.

So while this book is not about emergency savings, saving money for short-term needs, or debt, they are areas of your financial life that need to be taken care in advance of or requisite to your investing plans.

Saving vs. Investing

My focus for *Real World Investing* [this book] is investing, not savings. Yet in daily life I often interchange the words. I'll likely interchange the words here, too. So perhaps it is a good idea to differentiate between them because doing so will give you a better picture of the two directions your money needs to go.

The difference between investing and savings is one of time and the trade-off between risk and return.

Savings	Investing
Short-term	Long-term
Emphasis on return *of* your money	Emphasis on return *on* your money

With either savings or investing you are saving money... putting it aside for a later use. A good way to remember savings is to consider it "safe"-ing the money... making and keeping it safe. By safe I mean that it will not go down in value to any appreciable degree, even in the short-term. In fact, that is probably why you are "safe"-ing the money: the need for the money is a short time away and you can't afford for it to be down when you need it.

Why does time matter? Because most all of the investments we will consider have the tendency to go down during certain economic events. We call these "at-risk" investments. The reason we use them is because that while there is a potential for a short-term downside, what you are really after is the long-term growth they will give. But what if you don't have a long-term? What if you need the money tomorrow or next year? Having that sort of money in at-risk investments is akin to gambling. If you have a bad spell in the market, you might not have time for the investments to recover their value before you need to spend the money.

For example, let's say that in the year 2007, you had $30,000 saved up for a car you were planning to buy in 2009. While you could get a quite adequate car for that amount, you knew that the stock market averages around 10% each year in return. Well, in a couple years that $30,000 could be worth more than $36,000... you could get a nicer car. So you put your car savings into the stock market. And two years later you had less than $15,000.

That is why you want safe investments for short-term goals. You give up long-term returns for safety. That's the tradeoff. Bank accounts, after all, don't average 10% a year. That's a fair tradeoff as you do don't have the time to wait. Yes, you might earn next to nothing on your money... but at least it will be there when you need it.

Savings is mostly for those items you know are going to cost more than what fits into your normal monthly budget. If you drive, this is your next car (or at least a sizeable down payment). If you have a house, this is where money for the next roof and air conditioner comes from. It might be for a special trip you want to take. But it is also for the mundane items like maintenance and repairs on the stuff you own.

Debt – the killer

Debt is a cash-flow killer. While it may make things easier at first, you are essentially borrowing tomorrow's income today... at interest. You'll then have to spend less in the future to make up the difference. If you thought things were bad now, pushing your problems into the future is not a good answer. Sometimes it is necessary, but it should be the exception rather than the rule. Keeping up your standard of living now by creating debt will lower your standard of living in the future.

Using debt is also presumptive. At least if you spend today's money today you know that you have it to spend. If you spend tomorrow's money today, you are assuming that the money will be there tomorrow. Sometimes it is, and sometimes it isn't.

A good way to look at debt is to think of it as savings, but in reverse. When you save, you put money aside, maybe earn a little interest, and then you buy what you want. With debt, you buy what you want now, end up paying a lot of interest, and then you "save" the money by paying down your debt.

Imagine your road to investing as a real-life number line. With numbers, before you can go positive you need to get out of the negative. So your first steps on your journey are to get your debt to a manageable point. Manageable means you have enough set aside to pay off your debt or you have enough guaranteed income to make your debt payments.

What I've been talking about mostly applies to things like car loans and credit cards. And while a house is more of an investment, if you borrow to afford it (and most of us do) then the same applies. You'll want to either have money in your other investments to be able to pay off the house loan, or enough income to make your debt payments without straining your budget or ignoring other parts of your savings program.

EMERGENCY FUND – FOR THE 'WHAT-IFS' IN LIFE

The first way to protect against the risk of the unexpected is to build up some emergency funds. (You can call them emergency, contingency, or rainy-day... it's all the same to me.)

This is the building block of all other savings and investing programs. The emergency fund keeps the debts from piling up, allows you to use timed deposits (think CDs) and riskier assets in other areas, and gives peace of mind.

No emergency fund? While you may not want to think about the surprisingly bad and expensive things that can happen in life, assuming things will go as planned relies on hope, not realism.

How much is enough?

- Enough to handle "general" emergencies like a broken refrigerator, car accident, or a trip to visit a sick relative.
- Enough to handle medical emergencies. In other words, enough to cover your maximum annual out-of-pocket cost under your health insurance.
- Enough to handle other big expenses that you had savings plans for but that came early. As a minimum this is where the money comes from to pay expenses that your auto or home insurance deductible won't pay.
- Enough to last 6-12 months without a job.

That last one can take a lot of money. So I don't mind you paralleling that build-up of funds with the start of your investing program. With care they can play double-duty.

INSURANCE

The second way is to protect against risk is by purchasing an adequate mix of insurance that will cover your property, and help you through a period of sickness or disability. Life insurance falls under this as well. But in this case we don't care about the amount held on your life... if you're dead, you really don't need much money. Instead we want to make sure there is enough coverage on whomever you are dependent upon for income. Usually this is a spouse, but in a business it may be a co-owner or key employee.

Of course, your spouse will want the same for you.

Any of the problems that these types of insurance protect against can derail your savings plans or empty out your investments prematurely. You are, through insurance, transferring most of the risk of one of these unlikely "problems" messing you up from your pocketbook to that of the insurance company.

Many folks will forgo insurance completely or under-insure because they think it is a waste of money. Here's the thing: You HOPE it is a waste of money. Insurance pays the economic cost of some tragedies of life. I'd rather the insurance company keeps the money and I never have the tragedy.

CHAPTER 2
Planing and Goal Creation

"*If you don't know where you are going, you might wind up someplace else.*"
–Yogi Berra

Many people invest money for reasons that have no true meaning for them. If instead you began by focusing in on what matters to you in life and ensure that your priorities (goals) are consistent with those matters, then your investments will, in turn, support what is truly important to you.

Why are you investing? If you tell me, "Well, I just want more money," I'll ask, "What are you planning to spend that money on?" Before you begin investing you need to ask yourself why those investments matter to you. To get the answer, I suggest following a three-tiered process of planning.

LEVELS OF PLANNING

There is a hierarchy in your planning. We don't begin by planning investments. Your investment goal isn't there for its own sake. Rather, it supports one or more of your financial goals. Likewise, financial goals aren't there for themselves. Instead, they support your life goals. Each must be based on the planning before it.

LIFE PLANNING -

What are you trying to do in life?

FINANCIAL PLANNING -

What are the financial needs of your life goals?

INVESTMENT PLANNING -

What are the investment needs of your financial goals?

Not all life goals need financial goals to support them, just as not all financial goals require investing. But every investment goal has an associated financial goal and every financial goal has an associated life goal. At least they should.

THE GOAL OF YOUR GOALS

When you are done with your goals, you should know...

- Why you are investing your money.
- When you will first need the money.
- When you no longer need the money.
- If you have any "slop" in your goal.

Some of your "whys" will be dreams, some will be wants, and some will be needs. But they all will be important to you.

Here's an example to clarify things. One of my life planning goals is to have shelter that keeps my family safe and comfortable. I want it to be done in a way where it does not add significantly to my stress (I get enough of that from the business). I say shelter because I don't want to make a house mandatory. An apartment or even a cruise ship might make sense one day. But for now our family satisfies this requirement with a house.

I have a philosophy that is germane to this goal, and that is if I'll need to do something later in order to sell the house, I want to do it now when I can enjoy it too. To that end I'd like to redo a bathroom sooner than later.

That life goal of shelter leads to the financial goal of having enough in resources to redo the bathroom. This goal has some slop in it. An "adequate" updating will cost around $5000. One that matches my wants would run around $10,000. The timing also has some leeway. While doing it right now is fine, waiting a few years is fine as well.

That then leads to my investment goal. I'm looking for an investment that is expected to grow to $5000 within the next 3-5 years as a minimum. I also know that I have a fairly high tolerance for risk, so if I save $6000 across the next five years, but end up losing money, as long as my balance is at least $5000 come remodel time, I'm fine with that.

Given that information I can then look into how much I already have saved, what my budget can handle as far as additions each month, and the type of investment(s) I might use.

COMMON LIFE GOALS FOR VARIOUS AGE GROUPS

Need some help getting started? While no two people are the same, we find similar needs and goals among people as they grow through life and to retirement.

Age Groups and their Common Goals

Ages 25-35
- Provide support for children
- Improve housing
- Focus on career goals
- Increase credit limit
- Purchase insurance for household
- Establish fund for children's education

- Start savings/investment program
- Make wills

Ages 36-50

- Change/upgrade work situation
- Add to education fund
- Increase insurance for head of household
- Establish retirement goals
- Analyze/revise investments
- Update retirement goals
- Update wills/estate plans
- Maintain savings/investment program
- Plan for future security

Ages 51-65

- Evaluate financial assets
- Establish retirement plans
- Provide for aging parents
- Adjust spending habits
- Begin new lifestyle
- Update wills/estate plans

Age 65+

- Shift from money flowing into investment to money flowing out.
- Help grandkids get started.
- Establish a legacy.

GOAL SETTING: TIPS FOR SUCCESS

When you set financial goals, keep three things in mind:

BE REALISTIC:

Set goals that make sense and are possible for you to achieve. Sometimes you will have to accomplish short term goals before you can make long term plans.

BE SPECIFIC:

Set target dates for reaching your goals. Attach dollar amounts to you goals. This will help you monitor your progress.

VISUALIZE YOUR GOALS:

Think about your goals often. Imagine yourself achieving your goals. This will increase your desire to succeed.

Investing is not about maximum returns, it's about matching your returns (and the risks associated with them) to your goals.

Now that we've introduced goal setting in the next chapter we will develop investment goals and use them to build your investment strategy.

CHAPTER 3

Applying Your Goals To Your Investment Strategy

Once you know your financial goals (remember: that comes after you know your life goals), it's time to start your investment plan. Because this is part of a planned purpose, we are not exclusively focused on generating the best returns. Rather, you should follow a strategy that
- will give you a reasonable return,
- at a reasonable risk,
- and provide for your goals.

WHAT ARE YOUR GOALS?

As we discussed one of the most important things you can do when planning, maintaining, revisiting, or just plain worrying about your investments is to consider why you are investing in the first place. For example, you could be saving your money for a dream vacation. But it's more than just "what." There's also the "when", the "why", the "how", and the "who."

WHY

Let's start with the "why." "We wanted to see the Mediterranean and thought a cruise might be nice." This reasoning may indicate that the exact cost of the trip, as well as the timing, may be flexible.

HOW (MUCH)

This, of course, leads to the how...or more specifically, "how much?" Combining the why and the how might tell me that while your dream vacation would be $10,000, you'd have a great time and be quite satisfied if you took the $5000 cruise.

WHO

The Who is a rock band. But, in our context "who" refers to yourself and the others who will be managing and monitoring the investments that will get you to your goal. How much investing experience do they have? If you are handling the investing yourself, how much tolerance do you have for the ups and downs of the market? Do you get excited and dump more money in when the markets are going up, only to get scared and yank it out when it goes down? We all have our limits. What are yours?

WHEN

It's important to know the "when." There's not enough time for any risky investment to bounce back if we have a market dip before your vacation next summer, so here you might want the protection of a bank CD. But if you are planning a celebratory retirement vacation that's 15 years from now, investments including equities and corporate bonds have enough time to recover from short-term losses.

PUTTING IT TOGETHER

Knowing the what, how, why, who, and when, of your goals for a particular investment will help keep you focused and on track, and less likely to make common investing mistakes. For instance, when you get that "hot" tip from your cousin about an Indonesian stock that can't fail to hit it big, you can review your goals. In doing so, you might note that your trip is now 5 years away. You know that 5 years is not a long time when it comes to stocks and that while you will very likely make money, there's about a 20% chance that you might not.

You and your spouse may have decided that the 5-year mark is not set in stone. If the vacation wasn't until year 7 or 8 you would both be fine with that. Maybe the stock tip will help. You would both need to consider your tolerance for risk and decide if delaying or even missing out on the trip is worth the risk. Because you've considered the what, when, why, how and who or your goals, you are less likely to deviate from the plans you've made to get you there.

UNDERSTANDING THE MARKET'S ROLE IN YOUR GOALS

MARKET KNOWLEDGE IS POWER

So now we know that: 1) you have a reason you are saving and investing money, and 2) you need to keep that reason in mind in order to manage your investments successfully.

I'll let you in on a little secret about how to meet your goals: You have to keep the markets from surprising you. Before I go on, we need to define surprise. The best way to do this is with a real-life example. From their highs toward the end of 2007, many of the stock indexes dropped over 50% during the Financial Crisis. In March of 2009, the stock markets hit their bottom. More than half of people's wealth that had been invested in equities was gone.

I was not surprised.

That doesn't mean that I predicted the decline, sold all my clients' stocks and hid the money in a bank account and missed the bear market. I did not know when the decline would happen, but I was not surprised. I didn't know just how bad this particular market was going to become, but again I was not surprised.

I was in the minority. Many people were shocked by how far the market could decline, including many of my fellow professionals.

Likewise I did not know that the market would more than double from that March bottom in just a few short years. Yet, still, I was not surprised.

Good surgeons are not surprised when the unexpected happens in surgery because they learn about potential problems, and train how to manage them. Good mechanics are not surprised when a bolt-head shears off even if they have never seen it happen before. They have observed and learned from others. In the same respect, good investors know what the markets have done in the past, and what they are capable of doing in the future. They don't get carried away with the euphoria of the moment if an investment seemingly doubles overnight, nor do they panic when it plummets back down to earth.

If you don't understand what is going on in their heads, some of the world's greatest investors will even seem dumb at times. In 1999, many thought it was stupid to keep only a modest portion of their stock investments in technology. After all, why miss out on what was a sure return: 20, 25, 30% returns were the norm. Why keep any money in other sectors or other assets? Technology was royalty and the Internet was king. But when the king lost his crown, those "dumb" investors did not lose theirs.

So how do you keep the markets from surprising you? By studying. By going online, or to seminars, or to books, and finding out how they work and how sometimes they don't. Knowledge can prevent irrational exuberance and calm fear, allowing you to take control back from your emotions, and let knowledge and logic guide you instead.

Are you ready for all that work? No? Then hire it out— and milk the professional for their knowledge. Ask both the upside and the downside of any investment. Ask how it fits into your portfolio and why they think this. And watch that they give you knowledge and expertise rather than tapping on your emotions, just to separate you from your money.

You know what your goals are. You've learned not to be surprised at the turns the market can take. You know that even if you hire a professional to do all the dirty work, you are not an uninterested bystander. This is your life, after all... or at least your money. You are the one who will have to live with the results. And just knowing how the market works doesn't mean you're comfortable with it. You never want to invest in a way that has more risk than you can stand.

What are the risks and how do you know what amount is appropriate for you? We'll cover that in the next chapter.

CHAPTER 4
Introduction To Risk

> *"Some days you're the dog, some days you're the hydrant."*
>
> —unknown

UNDERSTANDING INVESTMENT RISK

Risk taking is invigorating to those who plunge down white water rapids, soar through the skies strapped to a hang glider, or descend into the earth while spelunking. For most, those feats bring not exhilaration, but fear. The same can be said when it comes to investing. Ask most investors about risk and you'll hear that it's something they want to avoid.

But what is risk? Technically, risk is simply the variation you see compared to the expected value. Another word we might use is volatility.[1]

Like it or not, risk is an essential part of any investment. Every investment decision, including stuffing cash in your mattress, involves risk. Your expected value is that when you come back home, the money is in your mattress. Variables include your dog eating the money, your kids spending the money, or a fire destroying the money. All are variables to your expectations.

3 ASPECTS OF RISK

The key is to understand what risks you are taking. That way you won't back yourself off a cliff trying to get away from a lesser danger.

THERE ARE NO RISK-FREE INVESTMENTS

To understand investment risk, investors must accept certain fundamental truths of investing. First, just like cash in a mattress, there is no such thing as a risk-free investment. I don't blame you for thinking there is, as folks in the investing world (me included) often use the term "risk-free" to describe things like bank savings accounts, CDs, and even treasury bills. But in that case what we mean is that there is little or no volatility or risk to principal. There are still risks that we'll learn about later.

---

1   Mathematically, investments going up more than expected is considered to be just as risky as when they go down...no wonder so many people have a hard time with math.

GREATER POTENTIAL REWARDS BRING GREATER RISK

Second, investors seeking greater investment rewards must be willing to accept greater risk.

But what if you don't want to take that much risk?

As you might expect, by lowering the risk of a portfolio, we generally also lower the anticipated long-term returns. This can be a good trade-off. Why? Because in time of market turmoil, investors will do stupid things if their portfolios drop too far for too long.

In both the tech-bubble burst at the turn of the century and the credit crisis that followed, markets crashed. In both instances investors could stand only so much, and many sold after the massive declines. If they had been able to hold on, they would have seen their portfolios eventually recover and grow. But fear overrode sense and their temporary losses became permanent.

This is not anecdotal. I looked at the Vanguard S&P 500 Index fund (investor class). This is an all-stock fund that follows the venerable S&P 500 stock index. It's about as plain-vanilla a stock mutual fund as you can get. Over the 15 years ending in June 2016, the fund has averaged a total return of 5.63%. This encompassed two very bad down markets and two very good up markets.

But realize what a fund makes and what the average investor in a fund makes are two different things. Investors have this nasty habit of buying more of what went up and selling when an investment goes down. Morningstar, an investment research company, has compiled not just fund returns but also Investor Returns; they measure what the average investor saw in the way of returns and will help us see the effects of the actions of the average investor.

So how did the Investor Return stack up to the fund's actual return of 5.63%? Not so well: Investor Return over the same period was a pitiful 3.51%. To give you an idea what a difference this can make, consider what a $10,000 investment can make in 15 years. At 5.63% that would have grown to just over $22,700 based on the fund's return. But at the investor return of 3.51% the account would have been just shy of $16,800. Since I imagine a lot of the fund's investors did nothing—just staying in and riding the fund up and down—it means that those who attempted to get in an out on their predictions of the future did even more dismally than these numbers show.

By limiting a portfolio's risk in line with your ability to tolerate it, we can reduce or eliminate the chance that you will "freak" and sell out during a market bottom. Preventing that possibility is well worth a slight reduction in expected returns.

Risk Varies by Length of Time

Third, the risks an investor faces can vary depending on how long an investor has to achieve her or his investment goals.

There are some interesting ramifications to this. Most investment professionals will tell you that time will reduce risk. But quite a few economics professors will tell you that the longer your time period the worse your risk becomes.

Which of them are right?

Both.

The stock market has a 20% drop on average once every 5 years. That's a risk. Sometimes there is a 1 year gap between drops. Sometimes there is a 13 year gap between drops. But on average it happens every five years.

So, if you put your money in the market next January 1 and pull it out 12 months later on December 31, you have a 1 in 5 chance that you will experience one of those 20%+ declines. If, on the other hand, you put your money in and leave it there for 20 years, it's all but guaranteed you will go through at least one and more likely several of those falling moments. That's what the professor is talking about, the longer you are in, the more likely you will have a nasty event occur.

But the investment professional is correct as well. That's because if you put your money in the market for one year, you have a 1 in 5 chance of being in one of those 20% drops and not having time to recover from it. You might endure a lesser drop, but enough of one that you're still at a loss by the end of the year. In fact, over the last 100 years, you would have had about a 1 in 3 chance of ending the year with less money than you started with.

If, on the other hand, you put your money in and left it there for 20 years, there has not been a time in the last 100 years that you would have lost money.

So even though the professor is correct and you will lose money sometime during your investment time horizon, that's not what you should be concerned about. Rather it is the risk of whether you will lose money from when you start saving for your goal up until the moment you spend it that you need to be concerned about.

AVERAGE WEATHER, AVERAGE MARKET

(AVERAGES VS. REAL LIFE)

Christmas of 2009 was a rather large event for my city of Wichita Falls, Texas. That "large event" consisted of several inches of snow that fell (and stuck) across the area just as people were driving to see their families. Hundreds were stranded on the highways leading to the city; the roadways were clogged with abandoned vehicles. The city was effectively shutdown.

I realize that this type of event happens only a few times a decade here, so it doesn't make much sense to have masses of snow removal equipment lying around. Not having that equipment, a storm of several inches for us is the equivalent of several feet in upstate New York (which I've also lived through).

Fast-forward about a year. That few-times-a-decade event happened again, and another time a week later.

Our citizenry doesn't have that short a memory, so as they saw the storm heading in, they emptied grocery store shelves and hunkered down inside their homes for many days. Accidents and rescues were down as a result.

How can these rare events happen a little more than a year apart, let alone a week apart? That's statistics for you. On average we don't see these kinds of storms too often. That could mean that a storm happens every five years like clockwork for an entire century. It can also mean that nothing happens for 90 years, and then we get a whopping snow storm twice a year for 10 years running. Both examples would have the same average.

The same happens with the various investment markets. As I'm writing this, over the last hundred years, there have been 20 recessions. That averages to once every five years. Recessions typically last about a year, which means there should be about four years from the end of one to the start of the next.

That four-year gap between recessions is the average. The reality is that of the last 20 recessions, eight were separated by two years or less from their predecessor, while the last three recessions have had gaps between them of about eight years.

So while the city and economists are right in using averages to determine how they are going to respond, individuals shouldn't depend on them. You have to be ready for one recession to be followed closely by another. Once you dig out of the current storm, you need to be prepared for the next. You also have to be ready when the events are 10 years apart. You cannot afford to be either an optimist or a pessimist. Either can get you into trouble.

Folks counting on stocks going up 10% a year were very disappointed by the first decade of the 21st century. Those who abandoned stocks after the series of recessions from 1969 through 1982 missed out on the greatest bull market for stocks of all time.

Expect the worst and you'll never invest in anything riskier than a CD, never start a business, never buy a home. Expect only the best and you'll get whipsawed by the markets, your business will fail, and you'll bankrupt yourself flipping houses.

In whatever is important to you, whether it be your vocation, hobby, or investments, you will do well to know what average looks like. Just don't count on it.

While risk cannot be eliminated, it can be managed through careful planning and following a disciplined investment process. But first let's examine the types of risks you face.

Types of risk

There are a lot of potential risks in the investment world. I think one time I came up with about 17 of them— and I was probably missing a few. If you've ever read the risk section of a mutual fund prospectus, you'll think you were reading one of those little folded up warning sheets that comes with a prescription drug. You know, the one that lists all the side effects that the pill has.

I whittled down the list a bit: Here are what I consider to be the biggest risks your investment portfolio might bring you.

PRINCIPAL RISK

One form of risk that everyone understands is "principal risk." This is the risk when you buy an investment (a stock, bond or piece of land) that it suffers a permanent decline in value. For example, if XYZ Corporation goes bankrupt, its bondholders may only receive pennies on the dollar for their interest-bearing bonds and holders of the company's stock could see their investment go to zero.

PURCHASING POWER (INFLATION)

A risk that many investors ignore is inflation or purchasing power risk. Even a mild inflation can damage your standard of living. For example, over 25 years (the length of retirement for many people) inflation will rob over half of the purchasing power of your savings if it continues at "only" 3 percent.

VOLATILITY

Another risk investors face is "volatility." That's the chance that on any given day, the financial markets might value your investment at a price greater or smaller than it did yesterday. With some investments, the highs are higher, the lows are lower, and the journey between the two is faster. Stock prices are more volatile than bonds. Small stocks are more volatile than large stocks. Foreign markets are more volatile than the U.S. market. Almost all investments are subject to the risk of volatility. Even rock-solid U.S. government bonds and notes fluctuate in value when interest rates move.

Now that you know what types of risks there are, let's manage them.

MANAGING INVESTMENT RISK

PROTECTING AGAINST LOSS OF PRINCIPAL

First, let's protect against the loss of principal. After all, any company can go bankrupt taking its stock and bond holders with it. The most common answer to this problem is to use short-term income securities like CDs, short-term bonds, and the like. But stocks can also get involved here. While a single stock can most definitely go belly-up, what's the chance of a basket of 20, 100, or 500 stocks all going bankrupt at the same time? Barring the core of the earth breaking apart, the chance is nil. (And if the core of the earth broke up, I guarantee the value of your portfolio will not cross your mind.) The key is to have more than one or two eggs in your basket so that a couple of cracks won't affect your lunch.

PROTECTING AGAINST INFLATION

Then there's the problem of purchasing power. Short-term government bonds and certificates of deposit offer little or no price volatility which protects your principal. However, over the long-term they have not been able to keep up with inflation, especially after taxes are deducted.

Bonds are a middle-ground, and a type exists that specifically adjusts to compensate for inflation. But if you want both protection against inflation and a decent amount of growth in your portfolio, the answer is stocks.

Stocks have, historically, provided the growth needed to overcome inflation and taxes. But their short-term volatility scares many investors. And as the markets have shown, "short-term" can last a decade. To get around that type of risk, you'll need not just many eggs in your basket, you'll need many baskets.

PROTECTION AGAINST VOLATILITY

As you can see, there is good reason to use stocks in your portfolio. If you have a long-term goal then stocks come into play as they grow your purchasing power faster than inflation and taxes erodes it. But with stocks comes some significant volatility. If you don't believe me, go on the internet and look up charts of the stock market. I bring your attention to 1987, 2000-2002, and 2007-2009 as good examples. Stocks are "bouncy" investments. And while a long-term investor can ride out the bounces, there is a way to calm things a bit.

That way is to diversify across asset types. No one investment does all you want it to. So, at our firm, we use stocks and bonds, from large and small companies, U.S. and foreign based, both emerging and established, and add in real estate and commodities, using indexed and active investments, and also throwing in some hedging strategies. Through extensive research and study (I'm in my third decade doing this and still spend hundreds of hours a year learning more) we mix, match, and contrast these various asset types to create what we feel will give the best return for a reasonable risk. This is constantly monitored and periodically rebalanced.

This process of managing risk, diversifying investments and balancing portfolios is called "asset allocation." It is, quite simply, the single most important part of the investment decision-making process. It is also a process that requires a careful examination of your goals, investment experience and tolerance for risk, your other sources of income, tax situation and a variety of other factors. Asset allocation decisions should be made carefully and should not be based on a "one size fits all" approach.

You'll also need some time, because with the exception of cash, any of those asset types can drop. And while it is just about impossible for all of them to do so at the same time, that impossibility happened in 2008. Even the perennial favorite of the masses, gold, was down in 2008.

More on diversification later.

CHAPTER 5
What Risk Means For You

Most books on investment planning dive right into what sort of return on investment you need to satisfy your goals. That's not how I do things. Instead you first should determine what amount of risk you can stand. For a given level of risk there is a given estimated return you can make, both average and worst-case.

After you determine the risk (which we will do in the next Chapter), and after you determine the resultant return (which comes from the risk you can take), then you will go back and see if that return will give you enough money to satisfy your investing goal given your ability to fund the investment. If it won't you'll need to change something (more on that coming up).

The reason I do the risk analysis first is that if you determine the return you need first, you are likely to talk yourself into a portfolio that will supply that return and ignore the inherent risk that comes with it. That can lead you to make some unwise decisions (which is my politically correct way of saying it can make you do really stupid things). The risk you can stand doesn't change based on how much return you need, it changes based on your brain; and most of us are stuck with the one we've got. It's a lot easier to change your goal than it is to change your brain.

WHEN RISK AND RETURN DON'T MATCH

It is not unusual for someone's risk tolerance and return needs not to match. What should you do when this happens?

RETURN TOO BIG?

Having an expected return greater than your needs and still within the risk level you can accept is a very nice problem to have. In this case you can either spend the extra money, lower the risk you take, or get to your goal quicker. The choice is yours. Enough said there.

WHAT IF THE RETURN ISN'T ENOUGH?

However if given your risk tolerance the matching return isn't enough for your goals, you have three choices:

- Invest more money toward your goal
- Delay the goal so the money has more time to grow
- Change your goal so you don't need as much money to fund it

Notice that I did not say you should take more risk.

In case I didn't make myself clear, I will reiterate: DO NOT TAKE ON MORE RISK.

Taking more risk than you can tolerate is not a valid choice. Trust me; eventually, it will bite you on the rear end.

SUMMARY SO FAR

Determine goal

Determine risk tolerance

Determine returns based on risk

Adjust goal as necessary

RISK TOLERANCE

So far we've discussed the concept of investment risk and managing that risk. In my practice we use a test developed by FinaMetrica for our clients. (Last I checked they'll let you take it for $45 at www.MyRiskTolerance. com.) I've found it quite effective. In fact it was the only risk measurement device that could correctly predict how both my wife and I react to different market conditions.

The problem is that this type of measure only tells us a portion of how you and risk get along. That's because there is more to risk tolerance than your emotional ability to handle risk. So let's take some time and discuss three aspects to risk tolerance that will give you a better picture.

CAPACITY

The first attribute of risk tolerance is Capacity. This is your ability to sustain a market decline without it causing you to reduce your standard of living now or in the future. This isn't a rich vs. poor determination, but rather an income vs. expenses one. For example, if your portfolio can reasonably produce double the income you need to live on, then you could sustain very large fluctuations in value without it affecting your lifestyle at all.

Capacity is the situation you bring to the table.

PERCEPTION

The next attribute is Perception. If you know that stocks often can drop 20% and sometimes drop 50% in a single year, you will not be surprised, therefore, you are less likely to be scared off when that actually happens. You know that stocks eventually go back up and that if you hang around long enough, things not only even out, but you make money. You also know that bonds, real estate, and commodities also bounce around. If you knew your bond portfolio could drop 15% (more if you were in higher risk "junk" bonds) and it did, again, you wouldn't be surprised. On the other hand, if you thought bonds were equivalent to cash in that they never go down in value, you'd be shocked when they dropped.

Perception is the knowledge you bring to the table.

ATTITUDE

The last attribute of risk tolerance is Attitude. It's the part FinaMetrica mainly measures. This is your psychological inclination to take a level of risk in exchange for a potential reward. Regardless of how much money they have and how much knowledge they have, some folks can't stand the bouncing around of the markets. Others are perfectly calm with the market swings.

Attitude is the emotion you bring to the table.

Now, your risk tolerance table is set

PUTTING IT TOGETHER

Capacity (your situation), Perception (your knowledge), and Attitude (your emotions) all come together to create your true risk tolerance. You're not stuck with your current capacity. By developing a spending, saving, and investing plan you can change it for the future. Perception is the easiest to change as it only requires study. Attitude, I believe, is the most difficult to change, as most of us are hard wired a certain way by adulthood. Even after significant market drops caused by the tech bubble burst and the recent financial crisis research by FinaMetrica, as well as our own experience, have shown that people's risk attitude barely budged.

Examples

To make this easier to understand, let's look at some examples. Please don't think this applies only to rich folks. I'm using big numbers because they are easier to work with (plus they're fun).

Best Case Scenario

Let's say that you have a portfolio worth $1 million, yet you only need about $10,000 each year from it to augment your pension and Social Security income. That represents only a 1-percent level of return. Even taking into consideration taxes and inflation, just about every portfolio allocation you can think of, from 100 percent CDs to 100 percent emerging market stocks, would produce the necessary growth to supply your tiny needs.

We can now look at your risk attitude to determine what portfolio is best for you. If you can emotionally handle the additional risk of stocks in your portfolio then you can do so and reap the extra returns. If you hit a snag (2008 being a snag) both your capacity for risk and your attitude toward risk will allow you to ride through it just fine.

A NORMAL SCENARIO

Then again, you may not have a pension, and your income needs are closer to $4,000 each month, or $48K a year. In that case portfolios consisting only of CDs, bonds, and other lower-risk securities will not provide the income you need, taking into account taxes and inflation. Here, you'll likely have to move half or more of your portfolio into growth investments (think stocks). Only moderate or high-risk portfolios will keep up your standard of living.

In this scenario your situation will not allow the safer portfolios. Your risk capacity shows that you'll need a portfolio with a preponderance of stocks in it and the risk (volatility) that accompanies them. This isn't a problem if your risk attitude can handle a higher level of risk; but what if it can't? This is a problem—and one you'll have to deal with.

In this second scenario, if you pay attention to your capacity for risk and put more equities in your portfolio, what will you do when the market cuts stocks in half? Your risk attitude points to your propensity to sell in order to cut your losses. Even if your risk perception tells you that you should hang on until stocks recover, your emotions will be driving you in exactly the opposite direction.

I don't know what you will do, but there are only two outcomes: selling and locking in a permanent loss or sticking with your holdings. The first will decimate your future standard of living. The latter will do the same to your mental health and potentially to your physical health for months or years. Neither are good options.

To keep this from happening, you'll have some hard choices to make. As I mentioned earlier, it is unlikely you'll change your risk attitude. That leaves your capacity. You'll need to change the situation you're in. And that means either finding other sources of income (not easy) or cutting expenses (not fun).

On the other hand you could do what most people do...just ignore it. In that case I suggest prayer, which is often a good idea, regardless.

CHAPTER 6
Rational Risk Reduction

PART 1: THINKING RATIONALLY

PROTECTING YOURSELF FROM THE LOOMING CIVIL WAR

An advisor I know got this question from a client: "How do we protect ourselves from the coming civil war?" Because of infighting in congress, massive unemployment, cities crumbling both physically and fiscally, this client was sure that civil war was imminent.

While I have not, to my recollection, gotten that question from a client, I have seen worry in many of their eyes...and actions. From wanting to get out of stocks due to the coming collapse of the U.S. dollar, to selling out of bonds in anticipation of China's pending fire sale making them worthless, to the age-old favorite: burying a bag of gold coins in the backyard for when society falls apart (feel free to use my backyard if you decide to do this).

Though I don't share in their predictions or advise their solutions, that doesn't automatically mean that they are wrong; and it definitely doesn't change the fact that they think they are right. After all, various political and financial commentators back their ideas on radio, television and Internet.

This lends itself to some potentially irrational thinking. Humans tend to not only listen to people who agree with them, but also believe those people are intelligent. At the same time, people tune out those they don't agree with and label them as fools or conspirators. While that is natural (I have caught myself doing the same sort of thing), it makes it difficult for someone to judge the merits of the various arguments on all sides of an issue.

When I was in high school, several of my friends were on the debate team. I'd see them continuously study these little note cards that contained facts about an issue (I imagine now-a-days they have a smart-phone app). "What side of the debate are you learning?" I'd ask. "Both," would be the reply. In order to truly understand a subject, you must understand the basis of the arguments from all sides, especially when the facts can lead to different and mutually exclusive conclusions.

Start reading the opinions of those who disagree with you. Understand why they don't see things your way. Examine how they can take the same facts and come up with a different conclusion. Learning the strengths and weaknesses of their arguments will help you learn the strengths and weaknesses of your own.

The scary part: deciding not only how you are going to act if you're right, but what you'll do if you are wrong. Those who believe Armageddon is just around the corner and have gold buried in the yard or hidden in the attic may be right after all, but have they considered just how they are going to turn their bag of gold into food, clothing, shelter, and medicine? I mean, if I had a cow and you were hungry, I doubt that I'd want to exchange my cow for your gold coin. I can't milk a coin.

By listening to all perspectives, especially those that conflict with yours, you pause and consider alternatives to your current conclusions. By both learning facts you may not have considered as presented from the opposition and by researching counter-arguments to their positions, you gain knowledge. Knowledge helps reduce your risk of doing something truly dumb, or will at least warn you of a potential danger that you can then hedge against.

PART 2: ACTING RATIONALLY

DIVERSIFY YOUR PORTFOLIO

Since there is always a potential danger when it comes to investing (actually, hundreds of them), rational thinking and the knowledge that comes from it proves that hedging one's bets is a very prudent tactic when it comes to investing. The fact that stocks produce the greatest return of any common investment type makes the retiring 66-year old want to put some money into the market. Rational thinking creates the caution that comes from knowing the stock market may go down almost immediately and may stay down for years. This then produces the prudent action of the retiree not putting all of their money into the market.

Most people know that diversification is a good strategy for an investment portfolio. In this post-Enron, post-Internet bubble, post financial-crisis world it has become pretty obvious that it is a bad idea to concentrate your investments in a single company or a single sector. Yet it happens quite regularly.

It might be a former manager who has 80% of her assets in her previous employer's stock. She's afraid of the taxes she'd face if she sold it. Another might feel it disloyal to a parent who willed them a small fortune in the form of stock of a single company if they considered selling any of it. Or it could be the packing line worker who knows the importance of diversified investing but who does not know how to examine investment choices. He places his 401(k) contributions in four different mutual funds—the ones that did best the previous year. An examination shows that all four of those funds invest in the exact same types of stocks. He has, in essence, purchased one type of investment four times. What he thinks is diversity is not.

That is why a rational thinker, in the absence of an adversary to point out flaws in their logic will do the questioning themselves. The former manager questions the wisdom of trying to save taxes in a way that might put a third or more of her net worth at jeopardy should the company falter and its stock fall. The inheritor questions whether the parent truly would be pleased if they kept all their eggs in one basket to their potential hurt. The 401(k) investor questions whether blindly choosing investments based on a single criteria is wise and devotes time to learn about what he is choosing or to getting good investment counsel to aid him in this task.

You'll find that rational thinking almost always leads to some form of diversification.

THERE ARE SEVERAL RISKS THAT DIVERSIFICATION CAN MINIMIZE:

DIVERSIFY AWAY THE RISKS OF THE INDIVIDUAL COMPANY

Diversification takes on many forms. First, we want to make sure that a disaster befalling a single company will not undermine your portfolio. That is why you should never put too much money in any single stock, bonds of a single company, or other investment tied to the fortunes of a single firm. This is also why most people should use mutual funds and exchange-traded funds almost exclusively. These pooled investments hold securities from dozens, if not hundreds, of different companies.

DIVERSIFY AWAY THE RISKS TO AN INDUSTRY

Next, you don't want to have too much of your money in a single investment sector. In the year 2000, the technology sector made the prudence of this approach clear. In 2001, airlines felt the sting of 9-11. In 2008 the anemic performance of real estate, auto, and financial stocks made this wisdom very obvious yet again.

DIVERSIFY AWAY THE RISKS TO A TYPE OF INVESTMENT

One step up from sectors are asset classes. The main ones are stocks, bonds, cash, real estate, and commodities. By properly mixing investments from more than one of these types of investments, you are protecting against large economic events decimating your entire portfolio. This is pretty obvious with even a casual study of the stock market in 2008. If you had balanced your stock holdings with those of fixed income investments like bonds you would have dramatically reduced the losses in your portfolio.

The mixing of different asset classes that tend to not be in sync with each other is what helps dampen out a portfolio's volatility. Interestingly some of the more volatile classes like certain commodities can have the most pronounced beneficial effects in reducing the volatility of the overall portfolio.

Diversify away geopolitical risks

Another area of diversification is global. The United States generates less than one-quarter of the global gross domestic product (GDP). This is pretty good for a country with less than 5% of the world's population. But we are not the world. Perhaps more importantly, while U.S. and foreign markets act similarly to global events, they do not react identically.

Certainly political and currency concerns need to be taken into account, but with over three-quarters of the world's GDP happening outside of the United States, do you really want to ignore the rest of the world?

Diversification has limits

Some folks say that diversification doesn't work any more... that it's dead. Their evidence? The fact that pretty much everything went down during the Financial Crisis. They purport diversification doesn't work since diversifying your investments in 2008 still resulted in a big loss.

Well, diversification still works. How can I say that after 2008? Because it was never trying to prevent a loss every single year. What it does is mitigate the losses. In fact, this has been proven recently. The 10-year period starting in the year 2000 has been labeled by some as the lost decade. Yet nothing can be further from the truth. Yes, if you look at the indexes such as the Dow Jones Industrial or S&P 500 you indeed made no money that decade. But if you diversified just the stock part of your portfolio to include small cap US stocks and foreign stocks you would have made money. Include commodities and real estate and you would have made even more. Mix in some bonds and you would have done stellar.

Proper diversification can increase returns and lower portfolio risk (well, to a point). But it is not a cure-all. When you get massive disruptions like we did in 2008 and early 2009, diversification alone will not help your portfolio avoid losses. After all, no matter how diversified you are, if pretty much everything goes down, you'll lose money. That's where having a cash-flow cushion comes in handy (this technique is covered in the do-it-yourself chapter, chapter 10) and why the time horizon of your investments is an important part of the goal-setting process.

DIVERSIFICATION MEANS NOT MAKING A KILLING

While we diversify to raise returns and lower risk, it does have its drawbacks. You will never have all of your money in the investment that does best any particular week, month, or year. So when stocks are in a bull market, any money you have outside of stocks is going to make your portfolio underperform. If the United States has the best market performance then any money diversified into foreign investments will be a downer. Yes, diversification will keep you from making a killing on any specific investment.

This doesn't mean that you are doing anything wrong. After all, for a long-term goal, you are not trying to design the best investment mix for today or even this year. You goal is to design a portfolio that will meet your goals across the time from now until you need to spend the money.

Not having your portfolio heavy in one type of investment keeps you from making a killing—it also keeps you from getting killed when the tide turns.

Chapter 7
Stocks – The Core To Long-Term Investing

When we build a portfolio for a recent college graduate starting her career, we buy stocks. When we build one for a middle-aged couple, we buy stocks. For the new retiree, we buy stocks. And when we build a portfolio for an 80-year-old widow, we buy stocks (albeit, not that many). Compared to bonds or cash, stocks have given investors superior returns and are particularly important in growing assets faster than inflation and tax costs.

Over long time periods, stocks reflect the growth of business profit: profit that every business person strives for. Because of this, stocks are the asset class best suited to produce growth over the long-term. And since the previous examples included a retiree and a widow who have a good chance of living another 10 years, I need to make sure that part of their portfolio will grow fast enough to keep their purchasing power intact.

Being hesitant to invest in the stock market is a natural, cautious reaction to the fact that the stock market can go down (and often does so in a spectacular manner). That is why the percentage of a portfolio invested in stocks is as varied as the number of portfolios we manage. For some people it's a clear majority; for others a minority.

> *"The real key to making money in stocks is not to get scared out of them."*
> —Peter Lynch

STOCKS: WORTHY OF STUDY

A long time ago, well before I began giving investment advice, and even before I invested myself, I thought that investing only in stocks was a wise move. The logic was simple. The common investments of that time were stocks, bonds, and cash. Stocks gave the better return: stocks earned 10%, bonds around 6% and cash 3%.

Basing one's investment philosophy on a single piece of data may be better than basing it on no data, but not by much. While those averages are still pretty much true, an average is, well, average. Those averages are based on multi-decade numbers. So indeed, if I had put my money into stocks when I was born and looked at the results now, I would be very pleased. My stock portfolio would have soared, greatly outdistancing itself from those containing only bonds or cash (or even gold).

But very few of us have 50-plus year investment horizons, and those that do tend to look and see what their portfolios do every year, if not every day. But even if they only looked at their portfolios once every ten years, that 10% average on stock can be elusive. For example, after the 2008 financial crisis you would have seen pretty much no return if you had looked at the 10-year average on large U.S. stocks—not a 10% "average" return. And I don't mean nothing for just the year...I mean nothing across the decade. Adding insult to injury, those thought of as "naïve" because they stayed away from sure riches in the stock market and had all their money in bonds would have seen growth rivaling what stocks normally do.

These weren't short-term numbers where volatile returns are to be expected. Short-term, gains or losses over 25% occur more often than most expect, but over a decade you'd think that the long-term numbers would bear out. That's similar to what I thought in my youth.

Since then, I actually have had my money invested in the stock market and have lived through a few financial crises, both personally and nationally. Initially, I gave my money to a "financial planner" (at least that's what she called herself). Imagine my dismay when she managed to lose half of my money... and do so in a bull market. Her concern wasn't for my portfolio—it was for her commissions. It seems to me that the only thing she knew about her recommended investments was how much she'd earn on each sale, or the trip she'd win if she was the best sales person that month.

My experience with that stockbroker ended up being a good one—at least in a roundabout way. Because she lost my money, I was inspired to start studying how investments work. I'll never be done studying. It's like walking to the horizon to see what's there... you're never quite done walking.

In my studies I found that indeed stocks return more than bonds and bonds return more than cash. I also learned that times similar to the financial crisis or the tech bubble bursting happen now and then. As most readers know, the stock markets around the world can drop over 50% in just 12 months, though thankfully that does not happen often. My education showed that bonds do indeed beat out stocks for decade-long periods occasionally. And I discovered that some years, cash is king.

At the same time a truth also emerged: Staying away from the stock market, even if you are in your retirement years, is just as unwise as having all of your money in that same market.

Stocks: Because You May Live Longer Than You Think

A major aspect of my career is to help people plan on achieving and maintaining a financially comfortable retirement. They pay me the same whether I put all of their money into stocks or all of it into bonds, so I have no incentivized bias toward one or the other.

The main reason why stocks need to have a place in your retirement portfolio is that you might not drop dead as soon as you might like. My preference is to do retirement planning with the assumption that the client is going to live until age 100. Most of my clients think this is ludicrous, but my reasoning is sound and based on actuarial studies. Actuaries are really boring people who like statistics. They work within the bowels of insurance companies, churning out data such as the odds you might have a heart attack while eating a grapefruit after drinking your coffee tomorrow morning. Their research is critical to an insurance company's ability to make money.

Those actuaries tell me that if I have a couple entering retirement, there is a 50% chance that one of them is still breathing in their early 90s, and a 25% chance that person is still alive in their later 90s. If you think that there is no way you can live this long, that's fine. We'll just assume it is your spouse who does. That way you are free to drop dead whenever you want.

Now, if there is a 25% chance that someone is breathing at around age 97, then I'm guessing that they are still eating, wearing clothes, living inside, and lighting and cooling that inside with electricity. In other words, they are still spending money. So by golly, I better plan on having money for them to spend.

Another problem with living to a ripe old age: Things will cost more when you are 70 than when you are 50, and they will cost more when you are 90 than when you are 70. While you may not see your cost of living go up every year, I think we can agree that keeping you comfortable tends to cost more over time.

Then there's one other itty-bitty problem. If you have investments and make money, Uncle Sam is going to want his cut.

In summary:

1. You (or your spouse) may live a long time;
2. You'll need more money every year to live comfortably; and
3. Not only will you need to earn more each year, but you must also be able to cover the taxes on what you earn so that you have enough left over to afford your cost of living.

What does this have to do with stocks?

STOCKS: TIME TO INVEST

Here I could dazzle you with numbers, charts, and graphs. But due to laziness, I'll summarize most of it. And I'll begin not with answering "why stocks?" but rather, "why not stocks?"

After all, stocks can lose a lot of money. In late 2007 through early 2009, stock markets around the world lost more than 50% of their value. As we learned earlier, that even wiped out a decade worth of stock gains. During the same time period, bonds, the likely alternative to stocks, returned a whole lot more.

So, why in the world would you want any, let alone a significant portion, of your retirement savings in the stock market? It has to do with those conclusions we came to earlier.

LIVING LONG:

Even though the stock market can be down for a decade, it's never been down for two, let alone three. So if you are 40 and planning on retiring at 65, anything you put into your retirement savings has enough time to grow to get over pesky little things like the tech bubble burst, the credit crisis, or even the Great Depression.

If you are in your 70s, you may be around another 20 years. You also have a significant portion of your future needs best served by stocks, even if the markets tumble early on.

In your 80s? Well, you might have another 10 years to go. And while there are certainly 10 year periods where the stock market is down, the vast majority of times adding a modest amount of stocks to your predominantly bond and cash portfolio gives a much better return without measurably raising risk.

INFLATION AND TAXES:

Let's use longer-term averages where stocks return 10%, bonds 6% and cash 3%. If inflation is 3% you effectively earn nothing on your cash investments. Bonds would generate an inflation-adjusted return of 3% and stocks would gain you 7%. Earning more than double the inflation-adjusted rate of return is good for your portfolio. Add taxes to the equation, and stock returns are stellar compared to bonds. Plus they actually get taxed at a more favorable rate than bonds. So bonds, after tax, might leave you 2.25% while stocks still have over 5.5% gain remaining—double what bonds leave you with.[2]

My study has shown that stocks should be part of a well-constructed retirement portfolio. Obviously, you need to learn more before adding stocks to your retirement savings if you're not doing so already. After all, you'll be the one that has to live with the results, good or bad.

Oh, and one other problem. Even though it makes perfect sense that stocks should be part of your retirement

---

2   The exact numbers depend on your tax bracket, the mix of long- and short-term gains from your stock portfolio, as well as the mix of qualified and non-qualified dividends

investment—maybe even making up the majority of your holdings—you may not be able to hang on to them. Following are some things to think about that will give you a full picture of what it means to be involved with stocks.

TAKING THE STOCK MARKET PUNCHES

Up to now I've been making the case for why you should include stocks, now let's shift to why a whole bunch of folks can't seem to hold onto them.

In almost everything we buy, low prices seem like a good thing. If a computer I was going to buy for $1000 was on sale for $700, I wouldn't worry about buying it. Sure, the price may come down more, but I am getting a heck of a deal if I scoop it up now.

I like cooking fish (the fish, on the other hand, aren't as thrilled about this). When I was picking up some salmon, cod, and halibut the other day, I noticed that the salmon was on sale. I put back some of the cod and halibut and picked up more salmon. If it was good the day before at one price, it seemed even better for a dollar off.

When it comes to investments, however, folks don't like it when they are on sale. Since the stock market has averaged one 30% down year for every five since World War II, folks see sales quite regularly. That the stock market has grown to 50 times its value since then is no consolation to a lot of people when they're watching their portfolio plummet that one year out of five.

This, I believe, is because of a phenomenon involving investments. If fish or computer prices are down, we realize that they may go lower. But we also know, with a fair amount of certainty, that the values are not going down to zero. Not so with stocks. People know there is a chance for a stock to completely lose all of its value.

While that is a valid point if we talk about a single stock, it is not when we talk about the stock market. A single stock can go bankrupt. Barring something like the caldera under Yellowstone erupting and ending civilization in the United States, it isn't likely that the companies in the S&P 500 or any other stock index are all heading to zero at the same time.

So, with my blessing, and your own study, you may start adding or increasing your holdings of stocks in your investment mix. But please don't do so if you can't stand what might happen next. The last crash wasn't that long ago. You've seen how dire the market can look. You've seen fear in the eyes of many investors—amateurs and professionals alike. The stock market will punch you in the gut now and then. Toughen up, be ready for it, and make sure you have a good defense in case of this inevitability.

That, or stay out of the fight.

PROMISES NOT MADE TO BE BROKEN (PULLING OUT OF THE MARKET)

I stay in the market because I can look at any graph of the stock market and see an upward trend. Still, look back at that stock market graph. It is not a straight line up. Quite regularly the stock market goes down 20-25% or more. Heck, we've seen it go down 50% twice since we entered this century. While making promises about investment returns is a big no-no to the regulators, I'm sure even they would allow me to tell you the following:

- I promise you that if you stick with the stock market it will go down. Maybe not this month, or this year, but it will go down again.
- I promise that as a result, your portfolio will lose money—at least for a while.
- I promise that you will not like this.

This doesn't mean you should ignore or enjoy market declines. There are many strategies to lessen the pain. For our clients we used a variety of methods to try and minimize the downside of their portfolios.

The results? None of the techniques kept the portfolios we manage from losing money in 2008. I'm sure many readers used strategies that purported to moderate market losses and still they saw their account plunge during the end of 2008 and start of 2009. Yet I'm guessing that if you look at the history of those strategies, you will see that they never promised you'd avoid a market drop every single year.

But, in keeping with the negative tone, please concentrate on the sentence, "None of the techniques kept the portfolios I manage from losing money in 2008." That means that even when anticipating stock markets going down there is nothing that can be done to completely eliminate your losses if you have a decent sized chunk of your investments in stocks.

Nothing, that is, except to never invest in stocks in the first place.

Is that what I'm recommending? No, of course not (you HAVE been paying attention, haven't you?).

ROLLER COASTER MARKET RESEMBLES A STAIRCASE, EVENTUALLY

In 1971, Led Zeppelin released the song, *Stairway to Heaven*. This rock-n-roll classic has made Page, Plant, and company a whole lot of money. Here I want to talk about a staircase that can make you money...if it doesn't scare you off.

As I've already mentioned, if you step back and take another look at a chart of the stock market from before the Great Depression through the present, you'll see what looks like a diagonal line running from the bottom left to the upper right. That's because, in general, the stock market goes up—which is of course why people want to invest in it.

Yet take a step forward and look again. What you'll see is that the line isn't straight. Instead, it zigs up and zags down, sometimes violently. The Great Depression that my parents went through and this latest Great Recession that we've experienced aren't the only times folks have lost a lot of money. But a jagged line that looks like a ramp doesn't really describe the chart that well. That's where my stairway theme comes in.

Upon closer inspection, the chart of the stock market really looks more like a staircase than a ramp. The upward slope leading up to the Great Depression was followed by a flat decade-and-a-half. Next was another upward slope that lasted to the late '60s, when things flattened out again. Finally, the market took a swing up with the great bull market of the '80s and '90s only to be flattened out by the tech bubble and burst.

Back to my stairway: The flat sections look flat (at a distance) but they are a combination of both soaring rises and drop-like-a-rock periods. I like describing these times as "flat in an exciting way."

If you were to close your eyes at the start of one of these periods and open them at the end, you'd find that the stock market seemed to not have changed much: hence the "flat." But if you kept your eyes open, then you would have experienced a roller coaster ride...the jaw-clenching, white knuckle kind. That's the "exciting" view of "flat."

Take a hint from the Led Zeppelin guys; no matter the ups and downs in music, they stuck it out—and are still earning residuals from that song. You can do the same if you have their stamina.

THE MARKET ISN'T REALLY DIFFERENT NOW (MOSTLY)

Whenever I give a talk about how stocks, investments, investing, the markets, or the economy works, I'll inevitably get this statement from someone in the audience.

"Things are different now. What was true in the past isn't true anymore."

Now, I'm not a prophet or a seer, but I believe that what I've learned and studied is still applicable. Not believing that takes away everything that I use to manage money effectively. Therefore if you do believe that things are completely different now, then all of the lessons from the past 100-plus years (and dozens of these pages) concerning investing are for naught.

There is also no person you should listen to, no book you should read, no periodical you should subscribe to. They are all either basing their pronouncements on a past that some say doesn't matter anymore or a future that no one can be sure of.

As you may suspect, I don't think things are different now.

Let me restate that a bit. Things are always different. I believe it was Mark Twain who said, "History never repeats itself, it rhymes."

So, while things are different now, they are not too different from what has come before and therefore are quite manageable. Humans, it seems, do not change that dramatically over the years; and it is those darn humans that drive the markets.

"But it's obvious that we are about to hit a prolonged decline. It's all over the T.V., radio, and the Internet. Shouldn't we do something about it? We can always get back into the market later when things settle out."

It is obvious that we are about to hit a prolonged decline. It is also obvious that we have established a base and will continue with a prolonged bull market. It is also obvious that the economy of the world is in the process of reestablishing its equilibrium and we'll be zigzagging for a while.

All of these are obvious (no matter when you are reading this) because a great many learned finance folks are declaring it so. No matter what you think is going to happen, there are a slew of experts who agree with you. This is not all that unusual. They are all trying to predict the future.

Something else that is not all that unusual: those who predict the greatest doom get the biggest headlines. That doesn't mean they are wrong, but it doesn't mean they are right either. Me? I've always been partial to zigzags,

but I won't base my investing on that being the only possible future.

The Investment World IS different now (somewhat)

Now that I've just said that the markets are more
the same as they've always been than different, it's time
to discuss what is different (in a way) about them from
what our parents and grandparents knew.

I based much of my discussion and examples on what
the S&P 500 has done over the years. The S&P 500 is
an index of mostly large companies based in the United States. That itself is a problem. This is because the
country being measured (us) was going through explo-
sive growth during much of the measurement time. Now,
I wouldn't classify the United States of the last century an
"emerging" market, but it didn't act like a mature one the
entire time either.

The 20th century was a heyday for an America that
capitalized on the previous century's industrial revolution
and ushered in the information age. It also escaped much
of the destruction of World War II, especially compared
to what Europe and Asia experienced. And while I don't
believe the United States has stopped growing, I do believe that economic growth will be spread across more of
the world this time around.

Because of this, the S&P 500's history may not be
the best measure of how an investment portfolio will do

in the future. Rather, a much more broadly based investment in stocks (and bonds for that matter) is very much called for.

Market change is not a new phenomenon. Even something as venerable as the Dow Jones Industrial Average has changed markedly over the years. It has had to add different ways of doing business (Walmart, Home Depot, McDonalds), new industries (Intel, Microsoft, Verizon) and companies that changed business models (IBM, 3M, General Electric).

A generation ago, when I first got interested in the subject of investing, about two-thirds of the investible assets in the world were from the United States. That number has flipped. Now over two-thirds of investible assets are outside the United States.

This doesn't mean you should have two-thirds of your investments overseas, just as I didn't think having one-third made sense 30 years ago. Some amount of domestic bias is understandable—even recommended. U.S. investments tend to have better accounting controls, a more stable market, and a substantially reduced currency risk. But the old standard of few, if any, foreign investments just doesn't hold anymore.

As they say, the only constant is change. Don't be left behind.

Being Perfect vs. Being Less Wrong

"Being less wrong" is not a technique or a product, rather it is a philosophy. There is a lot of information out there to learn and understand. To put all of the information together and achieve investment perfection—buying at the lows and selling at the highs—is the Holy Grail of Finance.

I don't do this.

I don't know how.

You see, market movements depend on little things like supply and demand and how humans, their companies, and their governments interact with it. While the concepts don't change, the specifics of what happens in the real world changes every second of every day. There are trillions of interactions that occur between billions of people on this planet. Each one affects the world's economy. With all that going on, if you can figure out what the future will look like, let me know.

Chapter 8
Portfolio Building

The need to diversify brings us to a deeper discussion of asset allocation. This is the "how" of splitting up your investments so you achieve diversification. We talked about this earlier, now we expand upon it. And I'll do that by telling you how our firm handles asset allocation.

It may seem strange, but when we build an investment portfolio for a client we are not going after the best returns (though we certainly aren't trying for low ones either). Rather, we are trying to provide investment advice that will give clients a reasonable return, at a reasonable risk, and provide for their goals. To do this, our investment advice has certain characteristics.

For clients, this answers the question, "What do we do with your money?"

> *"Money is not the most important thing in the world. Love is. Fortunately, I love money."*
> – Jackie Mason, comedian

We don't begin with a list of top stocks. We don't start the process by pulling up the latest Morningstar mutual fund ratings or by predicting the direction of interest rates.

We begin with our clients.

We learn about them, their needs, their tax situation, their tolerance to the ups and downs of the market, and much more. Their goals become ours.

There are a myriad of investment strategies out there. Most are carefully honed based on long-term studies of asset allocation, rebalancing techniques, and long-term investment trends.

In other words, they are best guesses as to how to get the greatest long-term return with the least amount of downside portfolio volatility. That said, they can't all be the best, and some are probably downright wrong.

So, if doing this yourself, once you have figured out your investment goals, how do you go about constructing your portfolio? How do you determine what mix of investments you should have?

I don't know.

Okay, I do know how I do it. I know how several other investment managers do it. What I don't know is how you should do it.

Don't worry, I won't leave you there, but let me first discuss the portfolio construction process. At its core is asset allocation.

ASSET ALLOCATION

History shows that all asset classes have given positive total returns across time. They haven't, however, done this at the same time. Different markets and asset classes do not always move in tandem.

Studying the volatility and returns of the different asset classes shows that in combination they can reduce long-term volatility[3] without decreasing returns. In some cases, such mixes may even increase returns while decreasing risk. It's like having your cake and eating it, too.

This is asset allocation. Part of the process involves rebalancing the portfolio which is responsible for much of its benefit.

The importance of asset allocation in determining performance is well established. A 10-year study by Brinson, Hood, and Beebower, which ended in 1983, set out to examine how the investment results of 91 large pension funds were determined and why they differed. The results, published in 1986, surprised the entire investment

---

3 Remember, "volatility" is just another name for the up and down bounciness of the market.

community. Though many parts of the study are not relatable to individual investors, it did show that the mix of assets greatly affects the return of a portfolio.

Later analysis of the study confirmed this and measured that about half of the returns of a portfolio were due to the asset allocation mix chosen.

This doesn't mean that properly blended asset classes will keep you from losing money. In horrific economic conditions you can have a broad sell-off across most all asset types (think 2008). Yet over the longer haul, asset diversification will dampen quite a bit of your portfolio's volatility.

If most of the performance of your portfolio has to do with what types of asset classes you use, and in what proportion you use them, your first focus in building your portfolio should be on that, rather than market timing or individual security selection. Yet the hype and enthusiasm of finding that perfect stock, bond, or mutual fund tends to entice most investors.

Individual security selection and market timing still have their proper places, but it's clear from the available research that the asset allocation decision has the primary impact on investment success.

Developing an effective asset allocation strategy can become complicated. There are dozens of asset classes within the basic categories of stocks, bonds, and cash; each with different risk/reward tradeoffs. Nevertheless, proper asset allocation is critical to meeting your financial goals. I can't tell you on this page what mix will fit your particular situation, because I don't know who you are and your particular situation.

A guide may be a report from Finametrica and Money Magazine that suggested the average investor could stand the risk of having 56% of their money in stocks with the rest in bonds and other low-risk investments. Those who were quite risk tolerant could stand 70% or more to be in the stock market. Those with low risk tolerance scores could handle, at most, 30%.

VIABLE INVESTMENT STRATEGIES

There are many ways to invest your money. There are different investment types, different ways to invest in those types, different strategies for managing the investments, and different tactics for moving things around. For this discussion, I'm going to consider two viable ways to handle your investments: buy-and-hold and rebalancing.

BUY-AND-HOLD

Buy-and-hold is pretty self-explanatory. You buy an investment and you keep it until you need to turn it into cash to spend. This is a lazy person's dream. It also works out pretty well. After all, if you don't do anything in-between buying and selling, it's hard to make many mistakes.

That said there are two main problems with buy-and-hold strategy. First, companies change, and many don't

last 30 years. This can be fixed easily. Instead of investing in individual companies, you invest in mutual funds or
exchange-traded funds. That way you get a mix of securities in one nice wrapper and if something needs to be
replaced, someone else does it for you.

The other problem with buy-and-hold (and in my
opinion, the one that matters most) is that the portfolio
can get out of balance. For example, let's say you put half
of your money in a mutual fund that invests in stocks and
it earns an average of 10% a year. You put the other half
of your money in a mutual fund that invests in bonds and
it earns 6% a year. So at the start you have a 50-50 stock-
bond split.

Thirty years go by. You're now approaching retirement. Looking at your portfolio, you find that you have
about a quarter of your money in bonds. Your 50-50
split became 75-25 ...stocks are now over three-quarters
of your portfolio. Over the years stocks grew more than
bonds, so your portfolio got riskier—exactly the opposite
of what most retirees want.

REBALANCING

Rebalancing, well, rebalances things. You might rebalance once a year, once a quarter, or even every day.
Rebalancing gets rid of the biggest problem that buy-
and-hold has: your portfolio getting unbalanced. In the
previous example, the portfolio would have been driven
back to its original 50-50 split by rebalancing.

How do you do this? Simple: You sell off enough of the investment that is now over-weighted and use the proceeds to buy the one that's a bit short.

However, there is a psychological problem with this. If you were rebalancing once a year back in the late '90s you would have been selling off stocks during a bull market. Many people in that position would say to themselves, "Self, why would I want to sell down my stocks which are doing well and buy bonds with the proceeds? I should instead sell some bonds and buy stocks with the money."

Or consider this. In late 2008 you would have looked at your portfolio and seen that stocks lost about half their value. How likely are you to sell off some of your nice, safe bonds and buy some of those evil risky stocks?

If you're normal your natural tendency is to want to get rid of what has been doing badly and buy more of what has been making you money. So it is not likely at all that the normal person will want to rebalance in the right direction. Fortunately for my clients, I'm not normal.

I remember a phone call I received from a client one afternoon. Seems he had been looking over his investment account statements for the last year or two. He remarked, "I see that we've done exceptionally well in fund X."

"Yes," I said, "we've made a lot of money for you in that fund."

"Indeed," he went on, "but I'm concerned because it seems like fund Y hasn't gone anywhere in the last year... don't you think we should do something about that?"

"Absolutely, and it is remarkable that you called today, as we just changed those two positions around," I relayed to him. "Oh great!" he exclaimed. To which I replied, "Yes, we sold off some of fund X and used the money to buy more of fund Y."

There was silence on the other end of the line. That silence told me that he understood what I was saying: I had sold off a good chunk of the fund he was loving that had been doing so well and purchased more of the fund that was causing him worries due to its recent underperformance. I finally broke the silence. "My idea of how to make money is to buy low and sell high. Do you think this is a good strategy?"

We then spend a bit of time reviewing how rebalancing works in helping his portfolio not to get too heavy in any one investment or investment type.

There are many variations to this theme, each promising to fix the problems in either strategy. But I've outlined the main differences and problems that I've noted most people have with them. With either, you can be successful. Just don't think either one is problem-free. Now that you realize that, we can look at the specifics of how I create portfolios for my clients.

COMPONENTS OF PORTFOLIO CREATION

Now that we've looked at some of the basics of asset allocation, let's discuss how we at Personal Money Planning build a portfolio for a client. You can go through the same process with yours.

BASE PORTFOLIO

There is a base portfolio that I have developed over the years and tweak on regularly. It is my educated guess on what mix of assets will produce the best total return over the next 5 to 10 years. This is the core of any client portfolio.

RISK MANAGEMENT

The target allocations from the base portfolio are modified for each client based on a number of factors. One of the prime modifiers is their risk tolerance. I won't go into too much detail here as we already devoted a section of the book to risk. But so you know, we run the Fina-Metrica risk analysis on our clients before playing with their portfolio.

"The essence of investment management is the management of risks, not the management of returns."
           —Benjamin Graham

Bond Additions

Once we know our client's risk tolerance, we compare it to the risk we anticipate from our base portfolio. If we do not think they can stand that amount of risk (and most can't), corporate or government investment grade bonds are added to the portfolio to reduce the down-side volatility.

As you might expect, by lowering the risk of a portfolio, we also lower the anticipated long-term returns. This is a good trade-off. Why? Because investors will do stupid things in time of market turmoil when they feel their portfolios have been dropping too far or for too long.

Remember: in times of panic, fear overrides sense and chaos results.

By limiting a portfolio's risk in line with their ability to tolerate it, we can reduce or eliminate the chance that clients will "freak" and sell out during a market bottom. Preventing that possibility is well worth a slight reduction in expected returns.

Cash Flow

It may be the most critical part of the allocation process, especially as the client approaches retirement: Considering cash flow needs when modifying the portfolio.

Depending on client circumstances, the portfolio's recent performance, and the judgment of the portfolio manager, we keep between six-months and four-years of cash-equivalent and other lower-risk securities in the portfolio.

The reason for this is simple: Murphy's Law. This law humorously (though in my experience, accurately) states that whatever can go wrong, will. The first corollary to the law states that this will happen at the worst possible time. Applied to cash flow, this means that the markets will be stellar until right when you need to make a withdrawal to buy something; then they crash.

This then leaves you in a hard place. If you don't cash out some of the investments, you can't buy what you were planning. If this was a piece of art for the living room, it might not be a big deal. But, if this was to pay for your groceries next week or your daughter's tuition it is a big deal. If you do cash out your investments in the doldrums of a bear market, temporary losses become permanent.

Either choice you make is a bad one.

By keeping enough money out of the way of a crash, we can be sure that you can draw out the money you said you'd need when you need it without harming the rest of the portfolio.

Do we give up some potential return doing this? Yes. Is it worth it? Absolutely.

We'll cover this strategy in more detail in the DIY section, Chapter 10.

Client Restrictions

Clients will sometimes place restrictions on the management of their accounts. There may be a particular security that they do not want sold (or at least they want to discuss it prior to sale) or a class of securities in which they do not want to invest. In the case of your portfolio, you are your own client. So if you want to put in a restriction, I suggest writing it down so you don't forget why you are doing what you are doing.

Some examples might be to not invest in tobacco companies. Or perhaps there is a particular stock that was gifted to you when you were young and you have a sentimental attachment to it. Whatever the reason, decide in advance what restrictions you want to give yourself and if there is any event or circumstance that might change that.

Tax Management

It is after-tax returns that a client gets to spend; therefore we are always concerned about the taxes we generate in their account. We manage this in a number of ways. First, we encourage clients to use tax qualified accounts when they fit their circumstances.

Next, we also try to put asset classes into specific types of accounts depending on what type of income is generated. For instance, we avoid, if practical, using high income investments in taxable accounts.

If we can delay the sale of an investment and capture a long-term gain instead of a short-term one, we'll do it. But only if we feel it is prudent. After all, it is better to have a highly taxed short-term gain than a tax-deductible long-term loss.

INVESTMENT OBJECTIVES

Most people don't invest just for the joy of investing... they have a goal. Life's goals can create investment goals. And while we list this last, it is actually the essence of what drives the rest of our work (and why I started this book talking about it). Goals need to be carefully considered, mulled over, and studied. Doing so allows us to mine the information concerning the amount of risk a client is willing to take, cash flow that is expected, the restrictions they want to place, and their tax situation.

HOW WE MANAGE THE PORTFOLIO

Building a portfolio is one thing, managing it is another. And while there are some specific techniques that we use, what I want to cover is more the philosophy of how we deal with the ebbs and flows of the markets. Because I am as much an emotional being as anyone else, I can be swayed by popular opinion, become euphoric when I make a home run, and get dejected when my investment ideas end up in the red. To guard against making stupid decisions based on this, here are some of the things we, as a firm, keep in mind.

WE TRY TO HIT SINGLES, NOT HOME RUNS

I tell clients to never expect a stock, bond, or mutual fund that we recommend to go up quickly. It may, but they shouldn't expect it. We will often get into an investment well before it begins moving up. This is not because we want an investment to stagnate (or go down). Rather, it is because we don't know how to figure out exactly when a stock or the market as a whole will go up.

We don't think anyone does.

Instead, we look for those stocks, bonds, and mutual funds that on average give a good return over our clients' designated time period, which may be five, ten, or thirty years down the road. This is why we do not seem rattled when an investment has gone down. It is not that we like taking losses. Rather it is because we realize that investing takes time and patience.

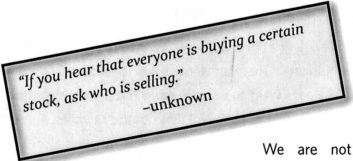

"If you hear that everyone is buying a certain stock, ask who is selling."
—unknown

We are not alone in this sentiment. Peter Lynch of Fidelity Magellan fund fame has said that most of his holdings saw their best returns in the third year of ownership by the fund.

In fact, the Magellan fund is an excellent example. Do you realize that under Lynch's reign, the Magellan fund once lost over 50% of its value? Let's say you had $100,000 invested in Magellan on January 1, 1973. Just two years later on December 31, 1974, you would've been down to only $43,000. What would most people do if this happened to their mutual fund? That's right—they would sell, sell, sell! Hindsight lets us know that even with this crushing drop, Magellan ended up being one of the best performing funds during Lynch's time.

The year-to-year variations in the market (and in your account) are not what interest me. What I concentrate on is creating a portfolio that has a high probability of achieving its goals. This includes keeping its volatility to a level that the client can live with, so that they don't abandon the course due to bumps in the road.

That's why we don't see "beating the market" as a goal we strive toward. We do not measure ourselves against a market benchmark. What we concern ourselves with are our clients' goals... both short-term and long-term. Our first consideration in portfolio design is to produce the return over time that our client needs, keeping the risk below what they can stand. Whether we beat the market or it beats us is immaterial.

Part of this is because there is no "the market." Rather there are many markets. There's the stock market, the bond market, the real estate market, the commodities market, the fish market, etc. And it doesn't stop there.

For within the stock market there is the U.S. market, the established foreign market, and the emerging foreign market. And within the established foreign market there is the Euro-denominate market, the Japanese market, the Canadian market, and the British market, to name a few. Not only do I not think it wise to pick "a" market to compare yourself against, I'm not even sure which "the" market that should be.

WE IGNORE WHAT IS HOT AND WHAT IS NOT

We won't invest in an area just because it is doing well. First, it must make sense as an investment. Next, it has to fit the goals. Finally, it should work in concert with the rest of the portfolio.

For instance, beginning in 1996 if you had purchased the top mutual fund from the previous year, over the next five years your average portfolio return would have been negative 2%. That's not to say that every winner turns into a loser—but it does show that trying to pick your funds by looking backward can be fraught with error.

Just as we are not running toward the hot asset classes, we are not running away from the ones that were cold last year. If a particular investment type makes sense for your portfolio, that shouldn't preclude you from adding it just because it's recently had a rough time.

Much of this is due to a concept known as "reversion to the mean." This means that an investment will eventually settle into an "average" return. If there is a mean reversion behavior for securities, then a period of great returns will most probably be balanced by a period of low returns.

No trend lasts forever. Cycles are a fact. When asked what the market was going to do, J.P. Morgan famously (and accurately) said, "It will fluctuate."

Here's a story I once heard at a conference to help pull this together: Imagine that you had to drive from New York to Los Angeles. You are in downtown Manhattan hopelessly stuck in traffic. Bicycle delivery drivers have been whizzing past you for the last hour. Impatient, you sell your car at a loss and buy a bicycle. Now you are whizzing by all those idiots still in their cars.

Sound absurd? Investors do it every day when they make short-term decisions for long-term journeys.

We also don't like newer investments that we don't understand. If a prospectus or a product presentation leaves us scratching our heads, we won't recommend it to our clients. This kind of philosophy would have saved many people grief in the limited partnership fiascoes of the '80s as well as the more recent problems with derivatives.

> *"The early bird may get the worm, but the second mouse gets the cheese."*
> – unknown

WE ROLL WITH THE CHANGES

My career involves managing people's investments and, on occasion, helping the do-it-yourselfers who don't want or need me to play with their money on a regular basis. As you can imagine, the world of investments changes every day. There is always some new fund, product, tactic, or strategy that I just have to start using... or at least that's what the salespeople selling those things tell me in the weekly phone calls, visits, and meetings.

But the thing is, while most of what is "new" isn't all that new or even all that useful, it is true that things change and I have to be ready to change with them. This is good for me and good for my clients. Because of this, I strive to improve continuously.

Since it is rare for a world-class economic, investment, or business expert to come into town, and the odds of seeing a major financial conference in Wichita Falls are about nil, I travel a good amount to keep up and keep ahead. Because of technology, I sometimes only need to travel to my computer, but there is still something about being immersed in a live group of your peers and industry experts that heightens the experience. Some of the best information comes from ad hoc conversations in the hallways. Besides, there is a lot to be said about getting out of the office for a while.

That's why I am sometimes found in places like Orlando or San Diego. Before you get jealous, realize that while conferences can be entertaining, they also involve long hours, a good amount of concentration, and a lot of homework upon returning. (Before you feel sorry for me, remember I was in Orlando or San Diego.)

After listening to some fantastic keynote speakers, sitting through a dozen seminars and workshops, visiting with well over 100 vendors, and dining with some of the most knowledgeable and influential people in my field, the real work begins. A backpack worth of notes gets on the plane with me, and I filter it down to about a dozen pages by the time I get home.

Even with all of that, I estimate that the changes I make in our client portfolios on my return represents less than one-percent of the money they invest. The small number has to do with the fact that I've been tweaking on things for over two decades, so each year the incremental changes are smaller. Although the changes are small, I go through all the trouble because improvement is worth it: a little improvement now compounds each year.

Continual incremental compounding improvement is not limited to me, or other investment dudes. Anyone can use good information from others to make small improvements in your own finances. That's probably why you are reading this book. Make enough of these changes and they will add up to overall improvement. And that's the best kind of change.

WE KEEP EMOTIONS OUT OF INVESTING

In the current Internet-Information age you'd think that all investors should do better. After all, anyone can find out almost everything there is to know about just about any investment. Why, then, have so many lost miserably during market corrections? A big reason is that information is useless when we let emotions interpret it for us.

Amateur investors base what should be long-term decisions on short-term information. They look at last year's mutual fund return or a recent earnings estimate on a stock and assume the trend will continue forever. At the end of 1999 investors could look back at the previous five years and see that growth stocks had grown much quicker than value stocks. You can guess what happened—value stocks completely dominated growth stocks in 2000 and for many years hence. (And, of course, they've flipped again... who knows what will be true when you read this.)

Taking emotions out of investing should be a major difference between amateur and professional investors. Yet sadly, even many "professionals" react emotionally to the ups and downs of the market. Star Trek's Spock is one of my favorite characters. I relate to him. So when I say I can keep emotion out of investment decisions, I mean it. (Though it's not always easy, even Spock was half human.)

But for most humans, making a long-term commitment to investing in stocks is easy to say but hard to live through. During a bull market people want me to concentrate their investments and ignore allocation principles. During a bear market people want me to dump their stocks and put everything into fixed income securities. Rationally speaking, "buying low" and "selling high" is a self-evident formula for making money on investments. But rationality goes out the window when prices fly up or plummet down. Because of this, investors have the tendency to "buy high" and "sell low."

This departure from rational behavior occurs because investing is an emotional experience. Prices go up—people feel confident—they invest more money. Prices go down—they feel scared—they sell. This is a normal emotional response. There is no problem with feeling this way. My gut goes through the same feelings whether I'm riding a roller coaster at Six Flags or the roller coaster of the markets. The difference is that I have trained myself to listen to my mind and not my gut. One of my jobs is to help my clients do the same thing.

WE KNOW ECONOMIC UNCERTAINTY IS CERTAIN.

In August 1979, Business Week's front cover declared "The Death of Equities." It was a bleak time in the nation's economic history. Inflation, interest rates and energy prices were at an all-time high, and 7 million shareholders had abandoned the stock market since 1970. "Only the elderly who have not understood the changes in the nation's financial markets, or who are unable to adjust to them, are sticking with stocks," concluded Business Week. Those that read and followed the teachings of that article missed out on a great bull market that lasted until 1987.

That bull market ended spectacularly on October 19, 1987. That day, Warren Buffet lost $342 million of his own private holdings in Berkshire Hathaway. Actually that's not true. What is true is that his portfolio's value went down $342 million. He didn't lose anything. He didn't lose because he didn't sell. If he had sold, he would have missed an even greater bull market that was yet to come.

Therein lies the secret to all investing: markets don't create losses—real, permanent capital losses. People making irrational and counterintuitive (stupid) judgments create real losses.

The key is to keep your focus on where you are going.

WE MINIMIZE TAXES

We try to avoid taxes, but we don't get ridiculous about it. We never let the "tax tail" wag the "investment dog."

Taxes are important... important to reduce. For the average American, taxes reduce their stock mutual fund returns by over 2%. We help our clients determine how to do their investing to save taxes. That is why we periodically sell some investments that we still believe in. If they have lost money by December and are in a taxable account we usually sell in order to provide some tax losses for our clients. We stay in the market though, replacing these with investments that are similar in nature.

But just because that is normally a good idea doesn't mean that always is the case. There are situations where it is better to take a tax hit one year than to leave it for a future one. Knowing your tax situation (and in my case knowing my clients') puts extra dollars in your pocket.

> *"The wages of sin are death. But by the time taxes are taken out, it's just sort of a tired feeling."*
> – Paula Poundstone

We also look at whether to use IRAs (Roth or Traditional), 401(k)s, SIMPLE plans, etc. Should we invest in tax-free municipal bonds or taxable ones that (usually) pay better? These are the decisions that we help our clients make in light of their particular tax circumstances.

But as we mentioned at the top, we don't let the tax tail wag the investment dog. It's okay to pay taxes. I know that few enjoy the prospect, but it is part of the game of making money. Some gains need to be taken now, regardless of the tax consequence. Enjoy the gain, pay the taxes. It's better than having the tax savings of taking a loss.

WE CARE ABOUT THE NEXT DECADE, NOT NEXT YEAR

Could the Dow go up 30% next year? Sure it could. Could it drop 30% next year? Sure it could. Both are improbable, but both are possible. So how do I handle this? I don't. It's not easy; we have opinions like everyone else, but acting on those opinions would not fit our overall investment philosophy.

Imagine an investment in which you have a 30% chance of losing money this year. Would you want a part of it? Probably not. Yet if I told you that it would average 10% a year for the next 20 years it sounds quite a bit better. Both describe stocks.

If you are concerned with what your money will be worth in the next year or two, then you shouldn't be in the stock market to begin with. You should keep that money in the bank. If, on the other hand, you want to ensure enough money is there 10 years from now—when your child enters college, or when you finally retire, or when you reach your '90s—in that case stocks can help.

All of this comes from our fixation on goals—what you are planning to do with your money. Financial success begins with understanding the core values and goals of our clients. I often get questions that concentrate on investment returns:

Why didn't my portfolio beat the S&P 500 last month?

My neighbor said the return on his investments with the broker across the street from you was three percent higher than yours last quarter. What about that?!

A friend of mine doubled her money in the futures market in one month. Why can't we do that?

These types of questions show that the client is looking at a short-term fix to their problems. Many people get caught up in trying to time the market; to find the next Apple Computer, or some fool-proof way to double their money in a year. Instead, we try to steer them to a long-term solution to their goals.

Getting irrationally exuberant because of market gains or panicking after a holding gets hammered is not a healthy way to react to the market.

We use asset allocation to reduce risk and maximize return in a way that matches a client's specific situation. In this we use both equities and other types of securities... no one type of investment is the answer to every problem. Using this investment process we build wealth, so that our clients can realize their dreams.

> *"Although the market may not always be rational in the short-run, it always is over the long haul."*
>
> –Burton Malkiel, in *A Random Walk Down Wall Street*

None of this is to mean that we ignore what is happening around us. When Treasury bond prices soared to the point that they were, effectively, giving a negative return, we paid attention. In our more aggressive accounts we shorted these bonds.[4] Though for the first many weeks this tactic lost money, in the end we closed our position quite successfully.

That's not to suggest we'll get it right all the time, just that we do keep our eyes open.

WE KNOW IT'S NOT ALL RELATIVE

Investment returns—everybody loves them. At least they love them when they are positive. But people being people, they get disappointed rather quickly. And some of that disappointment is mixing their expectations for absolute versus relative returns.

Here's an example of how absolute and relative works. Let's say that I won all but three of my games and came in fourth place in a one-on-one basketball tournament. That result of only losing three games is an absolute value. The fact that I came in fourth place is a relative value. Whether those results are "good" or "bad" takes a bit more examination.

Now let's take this into the world of investments. For instance, you might have been happy to own a mutual fund back in 2008 that was in the top 5% of all funds that

---

4   Shorting is the technique of borrowing a security and selling it hoping to buy it later at a lower price and giving it back. It is an aggressive strategy to be used very sparingly if at all.

invested primarily in U.S. stocks. That's its relative performance. Or you might have been disappointed to find out that you lost well over one-quarter of your money during that same year. A 25% loss is an absolute measure of performance—great relative return; lousy absolute one.

Likewise in 2010, considering the bloodbath you had survived, you may have been giddy to open your statement and find that the fund you owned gained over 10%. That's a lot better than a loss. Imagine your disappointment if you discover that the 10% gain ranked that mutual fund in the bottom one-tenth of all U.S. stock funds—great absolute return; lousy relative one.

I find that most people like to measure their investments by a relative measure when the market is up and an absolute one when it is down. This can cause problems.

In an up market, one of the corollaries of Murphy's Law goes into play—no matter how good an investment has done, my client will have a friend (or even worse, a relative) who had a better performing one. This makes them sad, so they call me up wanting to know why the heck I didn't have all of their money in this magical Fund X that their friend was using.

Then, when the market tanks, I get a call again. "How come my fund is down so much?" he asks.

"Sure your fund is down 15%, but your friend's Fund X is down 30%." For some reason, pointing out this fantastic relative return doesn't make them any happier.

It's just hard pleasing folks sometimes.

Oh, and about that basketball tournament: I don't know how to dribble or shoot, so while I might have lost only three games and come in fourth, that's only going to happen if there are only four people in the tournament.

YOU CAN FIND MONEY TO INVEST

I've had many people come in to my office and tell me that they don't have any money to save (which begs the question as to why they are in my office in the first place). When I ask them to show me their budget, they don't have one. When I send them out with homework to come up with a listing of their income and expenses, they can usually tell me where 100% of their income is coming from, but they usually can only track between 50-70% of their expenses. Likely somewhere in the gaping hole is the money they could be saving.

Often I find that small changes in your habits can create a good amount of money you can invest. Let's take my hypothetical odd couple, Fred & Wilma (Wilma's the smart one). Both work; Fred gets his hands dirty at a quarry and Wilma holds an executive position at a law office.

Wilma doesn't find enough time to have any kind of breakfast at home, so she stops at Starbucks and gets a Venti Caramel Macchiato (my favorite—light on the pumps, please) on her way to work every day. She wants to look and feel her best, so she gets a pedicure and manicure once a week. Wilma has been trying to quit smoking for years, but with her high stress job, she still lights up a pack a day.

Fred likes to eat, but he still "forgets" to pack his lunch a couple of times a week and "has" to go out to lunch with the gang. No matter how often Wilma reminds him to limit his red meat intake for health reasons, Fred finds it hard to resist temptation when he's out for lunch. Why not add the extras to the baked potato for a bit more? And who ever heard of too much bacon?

Fred and Wilma are doing their part to keep the local economy going.

Wilma loves Fred (we're not sure why) and Fred just adores Wilma. Their daughter is married with kids of her own, so now they can spend time together. They golf each weekend, go to the movies every Tuesday night, and have a pizza delivered on Friday when they stay in and snuggle up to shows they recorded during the week.

Unfortunately, they, as is common with most Americans, never got serious with their savings. They both have IRAs and a 401k plan at work, but are spotty in contributing to the IRA and only do the amount that's matched in their 401k. Well, we can help fix that.

No, I don't want to eliminate all the little things they do for themselves that make life pleasant. But what if we could cut all of the above in half? They could golf every other week, Wilma could cut back on her smoking (which could save on health costs in the long run), and Fred could still go out with the gang, just less often (and without the sour cream and bacon bits on that potato, which could help with future health costs as well). According to research my staff did, cutting back half on these little extras would save between $7000 and $8000 each year. For most people, "finding" an extra $7000 would make a big difference in their lives.

Looking for money to save? Try looking at the little things. Changing habits isn't easy. It might not be fun. But it can be worthwhile... and you're worth it.

Chapter 9
DIY Investing Part One

I promised in the prologue that I'd tell you how to invest on your own. This chapter begins that process.

WANTING TO BEAT THE MARKET

I loved those old TV advertisements with the talking baby. You know the ones—the baby is sitting at the computer trading stocks, bonds, and who-knows-what-else. When his Mom makes him take a nap he whips out his smart phone and keeps on trading.

What I love about the ad is the cute baby. To me it is a comedy—depicting a scene so farcical that it is funny. But this and other ads from different discount brokers also peeve me. They imply that, just because of the technology at your fingertips, even those as fresh and innocent as a baby can successfully navigate the markets and manage an investment portfolio.

Then there are the magazines, books, video series, seminars and workshops; all of which tell you that they will give you the tools, the information, to be able to wrest control from Wall Street and beat them at their own game.

Why would you want to use all these nifty gadgets? After all, putting your money to work for you is pretty easy, just buy a mutual fund. The easiest way to do that is to buy a broad-based index fund... essentially buying a wide representation of whichever market you are interested in.

But who wants to just do average? That's why you see all the ads purporting that with their technology, techniques, or "secrets Wall Street doesn't want you to know" you can get a leg up on the market. Anyone can equal the market by just buying an index fund; but you are special. With those special tools at your disposal you'll not only match, but beat the market. You'll see trends and data in such a way that you'll spot the winners and navigate past the losers. You'll be able to come out on top.

The subtle, and sometimes not-so-subtle, theme is that Wall Street is out to get you. They are evil, only care about their own profits, put themselves first, and are interested more in separating your money from you than in growing it for you. The only way to keep from getting taken is to get into the game yourself and take control of your investments.

I'm actually in partial agreement with this sentiment. You don't have to follow the news for long to realize that for many companies their profits are much more important than their customers. But the financial world isn't any different than other sectors of business. Car manufacturers and their dealers also want to maximize profits, so should you build your own car? The housing industry is the same, so should you build your own house? Thing is, some of you should. Some have the talent, time, and personality to take on a project like that and succeed at it.

The same with investing. But for the vast majority of people out there, do-it-yourself investing is not the way to riches, but rather to mediocrity—if not worse.

Instead of spending all the time, effort, and money to become an expert, I'd rather you find the professional that puts your interests first, who can explain things at your level of understanding, and who takes the time to get to know you rather than trying to fit you into a one-size-fits-all investment program.

And no, it doesn't have to be us.

TRYING TO BEAT THE MARKET

When you manage your own investments, you are pitting yourself against every other investor out there. What you are trying to do is exactly what investment pros try to do: beat the market.

Think about it: Actively managed mutual funds employ people who have advanced degrees in finance. Those people usually then go through multiple years of study to earn the Chartered Financial Analyst mark. During those years they are also working side-by-side with seasoned stock analysts using sophisticated trading strategies and complex computer programs to help guide them. They eat, breathe, and sleep all things investing. Fund managers typically don't have years of experience before taking the helm, they have decades.

Still, the average fund has a really hard time beating the market.

How then, exactly, are you supposed to do it? Sure, you'll hear of a person who does this all the time. You'll also hear of the person who always wins in Vegas. There's even a person who has won a lottery twice. But from what I can tell, those results are much more due to luck than skill.

If it was that easy, why wouldn't the mutual funds and the folks who manage the nation's largest pensions fire all those high-priced MBA types and just hire a few high school kids? After all, they should be naturals when it comes to picking stocks using interfaces that look more like computer games than research tools.

A ludicrous idea? Yes, and one that I hope will give folks pause before they start trading like a baby.

Now I'm not saying that a person can't become knowledgeable enough to pick their own stocks and bonds, or able to predict cyclical changes in commodity prices. But that knowledge will come from study and experience, not through an easy-to-use, one-size-fits-all technology solution from the discount broker with the funniest television ad. It won't come from a magazine that costs less than your morning latte. Technology can help if you know what you are doing, but it is useless if that knowledge and skill are lacking.

Actually, it is worse than useless. It is dangerous. It gives people a false sense of ability. Give me a powerful chain saw and I won't cut down a tree quicker, I'll cut off my leg quicker.

But there is another way to do it. You won't get to "play" with your investments, you won't be discovering the next great start-up to invest in, and you won't be day-trading. No, my alternative is rather boring. In fact, you can do this by having only two investments.

The next chapter will cover my idea of a way, a truly easy way, to do your own investing. And for those of you who really do want to go many steps beyond that and become like me, I'll give you my thoughts on how to get there as well.

Chapter 10
DIY Investing Part Two

Most people who want to do investing on their own don't want to make a career of it. They don't want to spend an hour or so after work each day in research. Heck, they really don't want to spend a day a year worrying about things. For them (maybe you?), I've developed this next section and while you can apply the principals to any goal, I'll assume you are saving for retirement.

DIY CHOICE #1: TARGET DATE FUNDS AND CASH FLOW BUFFER

Just because you want to have a simplified way of investing that you can control, there's no reason you can't emulate what I do with our client accounts. I still want you to diversify and rebalance. I still want you to be in the

U.S. and foreign markets. I still want you to have stocks and bonds and even more exotic investments. I want you to have a cushion of cash so that the whipsaws of the market don't affect your grocery shopping. And I want you to do this all by using only two investments. I want you to buy a Target-Date fund and open a bank account.

TARGET-DATE FUNDS

A Target-Date fund is designed to bring simplicity to investing for retirement. You need only follow two steps. Step one: Find the fund with the number closest to the year you plan to retire. For example, if this was the year 2017 and you are retiring in 10 years you might look at a Target 2025 or 2030 fund (they typically come in 5-year increments). Step two: Put (almost) all of your retirement savings into that fund.

Simple? Yes... well, sort of. Step one is pretty simple. Step two causes people some indigestion. After all, putting most of your retirement savings into a single fund seems to be akin to putting all of your eggs in one basket? You've already heard me preach to diversify. Fortunately, though it may not seem like it, that single Target-Date fund is already well diversified.

How TARGET-DATE funds work

Mutual funds invest in dozens, if not hundreds, of securities, so they are well diversified. The problem: most invest in a single asset-type, like stocks, bonds, or real estate, so the diversification is only within that single asset type. However, a special type of fund, the Asset Allocation fund, further diversifies by mixing many of these different asset types together. Problem solved!

Well, not all the problems.

While Asset Allocation funds are diversified across investments, they don't change their risk profiles across time. The fund manager is managing for thousands of investors who have hundreds of needs that are being satisfied by that single fund. Yet an individual often wants to reduce the risk in their portfolio as they get closer to and further along in retirement. In other words, people's needs-- and more importantly their time horizon-- change across time.

That's where the Target-Date fund comes in.

Target-Date funds, like any mutual fund, give you securities-level diversification—they own many of a particular security type. In addition, just like an Asset Allocation fund, they diversify further by owning more than one type of security. For example, they may include stocks, bonds and alternatives like real estate and commodities. What makes them different is that they take this one step further by changing the fund's risk profile across time.

People buy the fund with a date close to when they will retire, so the fund manager knows the approximate date that the investor will start using the money. So, as that target date gets closer, less of the portfolio is geared toward growth and more is invested for income.

According to the companies who offer Target-Date funds, this is the only investment you need for your retirement savings--for the rest of your life.

As you can guess, there are some problems with that one-size-fits-all approach.

A while ago I looked at a representative sampling of how no-load (commission-free) Target-Date 2010 funds performed in the midst of the Great Recession. These were the ones a person who is about to retire probably would use. What I found was that the funds held anywhere from 32% to 49% stocks and from just about no cash to just under 14%. That year those funds lost between 9 to 30 percent of their value. Imagine being one or two years from retirement and almost one-third of your retirement savings goes 'poof'.

Now, unlike the average investor, I really don't mind if a Target-Date fund loses 30% of its value right before the investor's planned retirement date. I know how to use a fund like this as a part of a retirement portfolio. I know the risks, and understand that the fund could lose money. I am prepared for it and plan around it. Unfortunately, the average investor does not.

Because so many investors with these funds lost a substantial portion of their retirement savings, the problems regarding them became clear: 1) Target-date funds with like-dates invest differently from each other, and 2) They all went down a lot more than people were expecting.

This is why the Securities and Exchange Commission (SEC) decided to study how ordinary investors viewed Target-Date funds. And they found that the ordinary investor was quite confused.

About half of the people surveyed owned a Target-Date fund. The study gave the participants information about a Target-Date fund in a variety of formats in order to measure what format worked best. Since most investors don't read any details about the fund they are investing in, these folks were already more knowledgeable than your average 401(k) or IRA participant.

Even with that, results were not good. Many participants believed the funds stopped changing their allocation mix at the target date and were invested almost exclusively in low-risk investments by then so the probability of loss was about nil. But the reality is that most of these funds will still change the asset mix (and therefore the risk profile) across time, and still use a wide array of at-risk investments at and after the target (retirement) date. The probability of loss was much, much higher than nil.

Almost two-thirds of the respondents thought the funds guaranteed income in retirement. No Target-Date fund has ever promised, guaranteed, or otherwise indicated that investors were going to get a steady income during retirement. These funds have a varying mix of stocks, bonds, and other investments. Some years things go very well; some years not so much. Yet many still think

these funds are supposed to be super-safe when they retire.

They were never designed that way.

While Target-Date funds do get less risky as the date
gets closer, they do not get to a point of no risk. That's
because, as I said before, most of these funds were designed to take you through retirement, not stop when you
get there. As such, while income is one part of the investment mix, growth is still needed. Your retirement will
hopefully last two to three decades. Living tends to get
more expensive in those later years. If you had a portfolio
that didn't grow, your purchasing power would shrink and
so, too, would your standard of living.

So, the Target-Date fund is there to provide growth,
across time, in your portfolio. It will have a good-sized
holding of stocks and other growth-oriented securities.
Its value will bounce around. This volatility is a problem
if you're at the point of living off of your investments. If a
year like 1987, 2000, or a 2008 happens when you are
retired and drawing from this fund, you would be forced
to draw money out when the fund is down. This violates
my buy low sell high philosophy.

Which Target-Date fund to pick?

Another problem with Target-Date funds, heck a
problem with all mutual funds, is that these are one-size-
fits all investments. They are not customized for you. The
investment committee running them builds the asset al-

location mix inside them to fit what they think is the best, most prudent, mix for people retiring on that date. They don't know you; they don't know your circumstances; they don't know your risk profile.

If you remember the steps I take in building a portfolio for my clients (chapter 8), to account for a client's tolerance for risk I will add bonds to the portfolio in order to lower the volatility. There's a way (to a point) you can do this and still use the Target-Date fund: Choose a different date.

On nice thing about using the FinaMetrica system (see chapter 5) to measure your risk tolerance is that they will let you know what a person with your score can tolerate in the way of equity exposure. You can then go on the web site of the mutual fund company you want to use and see what the equity exposure is for the various Target-Date funds. There's nothing to force you to pick a 2030 fund if you are retiring in 2030. So, if you find that the 2030 fund has more stocks in it than your risk tolerance can handle, look at the 2025 or 2020 fund and see if that matches better. Likewise go to a later date if the 2030 fund is too boring for you, that is, if you can handle more exposure to stocks.

Cash Flow Fund

To keep things going even during bad economic times, you need a buffer between your growth investments and your spending (between your Target-Date fund and your checking account).

We'll call this the Cash Flow Buffer.

Here's how this works: Let's assume you use a savings account for your buffer. Let's also assume you are retired and drawing $1,000 per month from your portfolio. Most people would have that $1,000 each month come from their Target-Date fund and go to their checking account where they'd spend it for that month's expenses. The problem is that if you are doing that during a period after a market crash, you'd be selling your growth investments (the Target-Date fund) at exactly the worst possible time. You'd have little choice though as you still need to eat and pay for electricity.

Enter the Cash Flow Buffer. Those draws would come from the growth portion of your portfolio and go not into your checking account, but into your savings account. You'd also have $1,000 each month come from that savings account and go into checking. The monthly withdrawals flow through your savings account.

Now if the growth portion is shrinking rather than growing you stop taking draws from the Target-Date portion of the portfolio. Since draws from your buffer (saving) still go into checking, your monthly spending is not affected. How long it is unaffected depends on the size of the buffer you keep in the savings account.

BUFFER SIZE

So how big should it be? I find that having between six-months and four years of cash flow works pretty well.

Yes, that's a pretty wide spread. But it has to be, as I don't know your tolerance. When I compared notes with other advisors regarding the lousy 2000-2002 and 2007-2009 stock markets, we had all felt very comfortable with about a year's worth of withdrawals in the buffer. Realize though, we all had 20+ years of experience and were all demonstrably risk-tolerant. When it came to our clients, the story was a bit different. Each one of us had a handful of clients that a 4-year buffer would be more appropriate in order to give them peace of mind when the world's economies are in turmoil. Where you fit in this range is something you'll have to figure out for yourself.

The more months of spending you store in your savings account, the longer you can go without having to dip in the Target-Date fund. The majority of time the Target-Date fund will make money. Most of the times when it's having a down spell and loses money you'll only need 6-18 months of buffer to ride out the down market. It is only the occasional protracted down markets that you'd need more.

Earlier in our discussion about risk, I mentioned a firm, FinaMetrica. If you took their test you could use the results to guesstimate a good buffer. If you were toward the center of their measure, 2-3 years is probably good. If you scored in the 30s or below you might be a candidate for that 4-year buffer. If you scored in the 80s then you can probably get away with the 1-year buffer or less.

The larger the buffer the less likely you will run out of money before the market turns and your Target-Date fund returns to pre-event levels. The smaller the buffer, the more money you've got growing... good for when times aren't bad.

What if you are a ways from retirement and have no spending that needs to come from your retirement investments? Well, that means you'll multiply your buffer years by zero dollars. So whether you're the type who wants a one-year buffer or a four-year one you won't have any money in your buffer. But note: If you want a four-year buffer then starting four years from your anticipated retirement you'll want to start building one up. The less buffer you want, the later you can start building it. A bit more on this further on.

SAFE BUFFER LOCATIONS

I used a generic "savings account" in the description above, but where exactly do you put the buffer money? Think of the cash flows that must come out of it. Some is needed now, some in a year, some in two years, and some after that. What you want is an investment that either won't go down, or if it does, in a worst-case scenario it is back up again before you need the money. Typically savings accounts, money markets, short-term CDs, and shorter-term investment grade bonds work well in here.

Do not shrink your buffer when the market is doing well. Do not grow your buffer when the market is behaving badly. Both are emotional responses to what is going on around you. Unless you've found a way to predict the next downturn, this buffer must be in place, and must be able to meet its goal in horrific economic times. Again, thinking that good times will never end is an emotional response, not a logical way of keeping your safety net.

This safety set-aside is really an acknowledgement of your mix of long- and short-term risks. In the long-term your main enemy is inflation—that's where the Target-Date fund comes into play. But if that is the only investment you have, you'll be forced to sell pieces of it to live on during market bottoms. This is a short-term worry and not one you want to ignore. After all, you've still got to eat.

BUILDING THE BUFFER

Using this simple DIY investment strategy, your entire retirement investment portfolio before, transitioning to, and through retirement is taken care of using a Target-Date fund and a buffer account. But there is a transition from the zero-buffer days of your youth till you finally get yourself retired.

Let's say you're 30 years old and don't plan on retiring until age 67. That's 37 years away. If you decide that you'll be well served with a three-year buffer, you'll look at your anticipated fund draws over the next three years. Since you have no cash flow that needs to come out of the account the foreseeable future, your buffer is zero and everything for retirement can go into the Target-Date fund.

Once you get to age 64, however, a transition starts. For the next two years you look ahead and see no spending needs, but in the third year, your first year of retirement, you are going to go on a cruise that will cost $15,000 and generally you'll need your investments to pay out $20,000 each year to supplement your pension and Social Security.

So your next three years of cash flow involves two years where you need nothing (since you won't be retired yet) and one year where you'll need $35,000. Thus you'd want to have $55,000 in the buffer for now. Each year you'd add or subtract as you look out toward your future spending needs. Eventually, you'll be retired and done with your cruise so you'll need three years of draws or $60,000 in the buffer normally.

There's even a bit of a short-cut you can take in building your buffer. Remember in Chapter 1 where I was talking about having an emergency fund? Well part of that was to have money available in case you lose your job. The closer you get to retirement, the less you need that part of it since, well, you won't have a job to lose soon. Those moneys can be repurposed from your emergency fund to your cash-flow buffer.

CHAPTER 11
Diy Choice #2: Becoming Your Own Expert

The last chapter began with two alternatives to investing without the help of an advisor; first, using Target-Date Funds and a buffer, and second, becoming an expert yourself. While the last section outlined a very workable way to handle your own retirement investments, if you want to learn more of the whats and whys of what I've been talking about, you'll have to do some work.

THE BOOK

When I have a new intern in the office, I hand over a copy of *Asset Allocation: Balancing Financial Risk*, by Roger Gibson, much to their chagrin. I tell them in order to understand how I manage investments, they have to read the book. Since the book falls right about 400 pages, they're not happy.

Does Asset Allocation cover everything a person needs to know about investing? No. But it does cover a lot. And I'm recommending it with some hesitation. It was written like a textbook. It reads like a textbook. It is as long as a textbook. It is even expensive like a textbook. But hey, if you want to learn by reading something, you could do worse than reading a textbook.

Most laypeople won't read this book, and most who try won't like the experience. Instead they search the magazine stands for a list of the "6 mutual funds for the next 6 months," or "stocks your grandmother would love." They want answers, not theories; solutions, not explanations. Unfortunately, they end up with answers and solutions that don't make sense for them.

I remember only one intern who enjoyed my reading assignment. The rest weren't quite as enamored. They'd prefer to get to the bottom line. I can't say I blame them. But the "quick fix" is like learning math by studying how to punch the calculator's keys: The calculator is the tool, but if you don't understand the math it's processing, you don't know if what shows on the little screen is even close to the answer you need.

Read Asset Allocation and you will know the characteristics of most of the major asset classes you can invest in, how they work together, and how, by combining different types of assets, you can tweak up your return and tweak down your risk. You've probably heard that you should keep your portfolio "in balance." Gibson knows that the right blend of stocks, bonds, and other securities that are appropriate for your portfolio is a key ingredient to achieving balance; in his book he explores how to do it.

The steps taken to get there sometimes seem counter-intuitive. For instance, if investment A went up 8% and investment B went up 10% and you mixed them together, you'd expect a combined return averaging around 9%. Well, that's not exactly how it works. Instead your return might be closer to 11.1% (read the book to find out why). Another example Gibson uses is to add a lower-returning, higher-risk investment into a portfolio. Why do this? Because it can increase the portfolio's overall return. Not only that, but adding in that risky investment can actually reduce the risk of the portfolio as a whole.

Learning investment theory comes in handy. For the professional advisor, understanding not just those weird facts, but the reasons why they are true, helps them build a better-quality portfolio. It also allows them to tough it out when everything seems to be turning to mush, like in 2008. Even with close to 400 pages, this is really an introduction. Learning doesn't come from one book, magazine, or seminar.

Is *Asset Allocation* too much book for most? Yep. Yet, if you are going to do your own investing, then you are your own advisor. Wouldn't you want your advisor to know and understand what is behind the recommendations he or she makes?

The point is that if you handle your own investments, schedule the time and budget the money to keep up with developments in the world of investing. It also doesn't hurt to be initially skeptical until what you read or hear is confirmed by further study and research.

Even if you use my Target-Date fund recommendation where someone else does all the asset selections and re-balancing, your own study can be beneficial. Even if you don't want to become your own investment manager, it will help you more fully understand what they are doing. That way you will be able to recognize when the results are normal or worrisome.

Either way, you'll have to keep the following in mind as you begin or continue to invest: Reality.

THE REALITIES

A client and good friend of mine took up the challenge of taking over his investments. He read Gibson's book and other sources of information about investing. He was able to ask any question he wanted as he prepared for the day that he'd become his own advisor. Heck, he probably had a head start because I think he's smarter than me.

But a year or two after he took over the reins of his portfolio I got a call from him. He wanted to hand the management of his money back to our firm. It wasn't that he couldn't be his own advisor, it was that investing just wasn't his thing. And in his retirement he wanted to do stuff that he found interesting and fun, not tedious and boring. Investment management isn't for everyone.

Still, the work he put into it isn't a waste. He is now a more knowledgeable client, has a much better idea of what I'm doing for him, and is in a position to protect himself from the frauds and scammers who sniff around wherever there is money.

CHAPTER 12
Dollar Cost Averaging

Up to now, I've pretty much assumed that you will be putting money into your accounts monthly. That regular investing keeps the gyrations of the market at bay. But what if you have a lump of money come your way? Or what if you have money already that's all in cash? Do you move this all at once to a more fully invested position?

I've been a proponent of the investment technique called Dollar Cost Averaging (I'll call it DCA for short). DCA is when, instead of putting a lump of money into your investments, you split that lump up into equal amounts and invest at fixed intervals.

For instance, let's say that Uncle Jack left you $300,000. You're worried that the mutual fund you use might go down. So instead of putting all $300,000 in at once, you divide it into thirty $10,000 blocks invested monthly over the next 2-1/2 years.

By investing at set intervals you keep from letting the market's emotions control you. By investing set amounts you'll tend to buy more shares when the market is down and fewer shares when it is up. In fact, if the market zigzags you'll actually pick up your shares at less than the average cost during that time (trust me...it's mathematically true).

That's the way it's supposed to work. Here's what actually happens. You start the DCA process and the market drops like a rock (sound familiar?), so you stop the DCA investments because you don't want to buy shares if all they are going to do is go down. When you are sure the market is going back up, you restart the DCA. If the market goes up rapidly, you end up dumping in all that you'd planned to invest at once so that you don't miss 'certain' gains.

Let's review: In theory, DCA helps you by mechanizing your trades so that emotions don't take over. You'll end up buying more shares if the market is down and less if the market is up. Thus, on average, you'll, pay less for your investment and generate greater profits.

In reality, you let the emotions of the market turn off your mechanical DCA strategy. You buy fewer shares when the market is down, more shares when the market is up and a lot more shares when the market is up ridiculously. This means you'll, on average, pay more for your investment and generate fewer profits, if any.

Don't do that.

That is, do the DCA, don't do the emotional response.

Another time-honored way to getting a lump of money in the market is to just put the lump of money in the market. "Oh, but it might go down," you say. First, you're likely only thinking this if the market already went down—a great time to dump a lump of money into it. Second, the market will, eventually, go up.

You could, of course, divine the future and wait with your lump of cash until the market is about to go up and then put it all in. Good luck with that. There is a two-thirds chance that a year after you could have put the money in the market, it is already up and you missed it.

So, if you've been given a lot of money and are wondering when to invest it, go ahead and Dollar Cost Average or go ahead and put the lump sum all in at once. Just don't try to second guess the market in either case. It seldom comes out well.

CHAPTER 13
Retirement Planning

Did you know that Baby-Boomers fear outliving their assets more than they fear death? That's probably a healthy fear because while they can't do much about preventing death, they can prevent running out of money.

In this section you will learn how to make your money last as long as you do. There is no trick, no investment you have to buy, and you can do this on your own without having to pay someone.

We have heard many people say they had to delay retirement or go back into the work force because of something "the market" did to their investments. The truth is that they were never financially ready to retire. Real estate goes down sometimes. Recessions happen. The stock market occasionally drops 50% and periodically has a decade with zero return. Inflation happens. And even bonds can lose money.

Frankly, it's a scary world. But with proper investment and financial planning, and management, you will make it through just fine.

Most people do no planning and have an investment portfolio that "just happened" over the years. They don't know what to do if the market goes up (typically they buy); they don't know what to do when it goes down (typically they sell). They have no idea what they are spending now, let alone what they will need in retirement. And they are doing even worse when we look at how they are managing the normal risks of life and investing.

I don't want you to be one of those people.

Up to now we've dealt with the investment side of things. That is, after all, what the book is about. Here we'll deal more with financial planning issues, especially when it comes to retirement planning. In this chapter I am just going to scratch the surface on some issues of concern. These details would take a book of their own to explain fully. My goal here is not to teach you everything, but to expose you to points you'll want to examine more fully, or get advice from a professional.

HAVING ENOUGH:

HOW MUCH DO YOU NEED TO ACCUMULATE SO THAT YOUR MONEY DOESN'T RUN OUT BEFORE YOU DO?

How much you will need depends on:

- Your cash flow needs (income vs. expenses)
- How long you will need it (life expectancy)
- What you can earn on the money (ROI) relative to inflation (real return)

CASH FLOW NEEDS

BEFORE AND AFTER RETIREMENT

Starting your retirement planning begins with your cash flow or budget. The easiest thing to do is to start with your current budget (if you are already retired, this is the only step you'll need). So get it out and begin another column. In it, mark how each income, expense, and savings item will change once you retire.

For instance, before retirement your income categories consist of your job and your spouse's job. At retirement, that category probably goes to zero, since, by definition, that's what happens when you retire. Replacing it may be pension and Social Security income, so add those in.

Expenses can change as well. You might be commuting an hour or so to work every day (not that unusual in my rather large state or a high-traffic urban environment). So when you retire, your gas and car repair expenses should go down. You may also need to replace clothing less often.

Other expenses might go up. You have more time to explore, so you might actually drive more. You may take more frequent or longer vacations. Just go down the list and adjust each line separately.

Don't forget health care. If you are going to retire at 65 or later, look up what Medicare and a Medicare supplemental policy will cost you. If you will retire beforehand and the company doesn't provide retiree benefits (or you are afraid they might cut them as many employers have) then see what COBRA benefits will cost. You might even be eligible for a supplemented plan on the government exchange. Don't forget to take into account changes in co-pays and deductibles.

And while you won't need a retirement savings category anymore, you will still need to save for house repairs, appliance replacements, medical deductibles, and a replacement car now and then. For now, ignore any money coming from your investments.

CASH FLOW PROBLEMS

DEATH IS A PROBLEM

This is especially true if you are the one who died. But at least your money woes are over. Not so with your survivors. When you die, income streams tied to only your life go away or are reduced. This will happen with Social Security, pensions, and the like. That is why I typically recommend getting survivor benefits so that your spouse will continue to receive an income. You'll have to see what makes the best sense in your circumstances.

But suffice it to say that if upon your death income goes down, then you need to look at how that budget will work for those you leave behind in retirement. If a shortfall exists it needs to be made up somehow. This is where life insurance comes in handy. Or you can start lowering your spending now so that if this happens, there is no deficit.

Oh, and Uncle Sam isn't going to help. A single person pays more taxes than a married couple does on the same income. It's quite possible with survivor benefits and investment income that your surviving spouse will be in a higher tax bracket than you're in now. Take that into consideration.

It is not a loving act to just ignore these things if doing so will require your spouse to cut spending by 10, 20, 30% or more after you die—especially if you're not willing to do so yourself.

Health Care Is a Problem

I have no idea what medical care in this country will look like or cost 10, 20, or 30 years from now. But no matter what it costs, you will either pay for it in premiums, taxes, or out-of-pocket. Don't forget to include your best guess as to what this might be in your budget.

This includes Long-Term Care.

Let's imagine that you have a need for long-term care, and it is something your spouse cannot handle at home. Long-term care facilities cost between tens of thousands of dollars or even over $100,000 a year (and can be even pricier). Let's say that your needs are modest and that it costs $60,000 a year. This is on top of the current expenses your spouse has.

How does that work with your budget?

If it doesn't, solutions such as insurance and Medicaid planning are called for. For Medicaid planning talk with an attorney; for insurance, determine how to fit the premiums into your budget.

"Guaranteed" Income Streams are a Problem

Okay, guaranteed income is not a problem. It's wonderful. It's dancing through the daisies, cherry on top of the sundae wonderful. But these guaranteed income streams have their own problems.

Some experts suggest having about 20% of your income in some form of annuity (explained in more detail below). Others suggest using an annuitized stream of money for basic living expenses: the lowest level of food, clothing, and shelter. Still others, though a distinct minority, suggest that anything short of 100% guaranteed income is just plain stupid. I'm in the 20% camp. For most folks, Social Security covers that and a lot more.

Three of these are the most common ways you get those guarantee income streams: Social Security, pensions, and annuities.

Now for the problems.

PROBLEMS WITH ANNUITIES

What a lot of people don't like about creating a guaranteed income stream out of an annuity (called annuitization) is that you trade your lump sum for an income stream and you will never see that lump sum again. So while you may never run out of money, you won't have anything left over for your heirs either. (There are some annuities that alleviate this issue, but have other complications.) That's not my problem with them. For me, it's the poor returns.

Poor returns mean that in normal circumstances you'd be better off investing your money yourself rather than getting someone else to guarantee future income. Usually a lot better. Of course this assumes the markets don't do anything truly unprecedented (what we saw in 2008 was not unprecedented), and that you actually know how to invest your money. But you're reading this book, so that's a start.

Another part of the poor return issue is most annuities do not keep up with inflation. If you start with $1,000 a month at age 65, when you get to age 95 you are still getting $1,000 a month. My guess is that it won't spend the same 30 years in the future.

Another problem—the guarantee is from the insurance company. What if they're not around in 20 years? Yes, there are programs to protect you... so if you go this way you should see what they cover.

None of this should be interpreted as my not liking annuities. They are a great tool to use if your situation warrants them. But like any tool you should read the cautions and warning labels before using them.

Problems with Inflation

The lack of inflation protection needs to be factored into your retirement budget. And before you wave your hand at inflation, realize the extent of the problem. A $40,000 budget today would need to be over $72,000 in 20 years to maintain the same standard of living if inflation runs a modest 3%. And a whole lot of folks think inflation will be higher than that modest 3%. In fact, if inflation was just 1% more, running an average of 4% per year, instead of needing $72,000, you'd need $87,000, and at 5% you'd need over $106,000. All because of a "little thing" like inflation.

Note that most private pensions are in the form of an annuity and have no inflation rider on them.

Problems with Social Security

You'd think that Social Security would be the ideal income stream. After all, it will keep up with inflation and it's got the best guarantee there is. There are some problems with this.

First, Social Security may not keep up with inflation. January 2009 saw the largest cost-of-living adjustment (COLA) to Social Security retirement benefits since the hyper-inflation period of the early '80s. And while seniors, according to The Senior Citizens League, welcomed the 5.8 percent increase, it still left retirees $216 behind each month (inflation adjusted) compared to the year 2000.

Based on their calculations, seniors have lost 20 percent of their buying power since the beginning of the decade. Across that time period, Social Security payments increased by 31 percent while senior expenses rose by more than 58 percent. Why the difference?

The difference is the way inflation is measured by Social Security compared to the method used by The Senior Citizens League. And while I can argue with some of the League's methodology, two issues merge to make the government's inflation indicator a poor fit to seniors.

The first is that the measure used is CPI-W. That's the Consumer Price Index for Urban Wage Earners and Clerical Workers. Guess what? If you aren't the average urban/clerical wage earner, the index doesn't match your spending habits. In other words, this isn't an index made to mirror the spending habits of our senior citizens.

The other issue is that most of the government inflation indexes, including CPI-W, adjust the inflation numbers due to technological changes. Here's how it works. Say that a standard television that used to cost $100 now costs $400. You'd think that the $300 difference is added to the index. Not so. This is because they subtract out the value of features you get in a television now compared to long ago.

These days you might get features such as a remote control, closed-caption, and an HD tuner. Since none of those features were in the earlier model, their estimated value is taken off. Hence that TV selling for $400 might be worth only $200 in the index. The other $200 of "improvements" is discarded.

That you can't buy a TV with all of those features stripped off doesn't matter. Cars get the same treatment due to air bags, anti-lock brakes, etc. In other words, the various consumer price indexes do not measure the rise in what a real person sees in consumer prices. This is bad news to anyone depending on government COLAs to keep up with the cost of living, namely government pensioners and Social Security recipients.

The other problem with Social Security is that it is not guaranteed. An annuity from an insurance company is guaranteed by contract. Same with a pension from a company you worked for. But Social Security can be changed by a vote of Congress.

'Nuff said...

Problems with Taxes

When counting on these income streams (or any income) don't forget to either use after-tax numbers or have taxes as part of your budget expenses. Drawing $80,000 from your pensions and IRAs won't satisfy your $70,000 lifestyle if you'll owe $14,000 in taxes.

And don't be surprised if taxes go up.

Live Long and Prosper

After all that, remember, I like income streams, especially guaranteed ones. In the Star Trek saga, Spock would often give the greeting of friendship, "Live Long and Prosper." When last heard from on the series, he was 139 years old. His father Sarek, lived 202 years. That's a lot of living long and prospering.

Unfortunately, unless you are also at least one-half Vulcan, you probably won't last as long. But you will likely live longer than you expect. How long?

Perception: People in their 50s expect to live about 21 years after retirement.

Reality: As was discussed in chapter 7, the reality is that with a married couple the average life expectancy for the longest-living spouse is in their early 90s... and what if they are above-average? They'll make it into their late 90s 25% of the time.

Do your retirement planning so that your money will last. And when you plan, make sure you use a reasonable life expectancy. After all, while running out of money won't kill you, it won't make you feel good either.

Imagine making this phone call to your child: "Your Mom and I weren't anticipating living this long and didn't make the preparations needed. We were hoping that you could help us, at least until we can figure something out." As hard as that phone call might be for the kids to hear, it is devastating to be one saying it.

In several studies the most common method for determining the amount of savings needed for retirement by consumers (that's you) is guessing. That's right; most people who 'know' they have enough to retire know this by instinct. No calculator need touch their fingers, they need not input information into an online retirement calculator, and there is certainly no need to talk with a financial planner. They just know.

WHAT WILL YOUR INVESTMENTS SUPPORT?

THE 4% RULE

Don't guess. To know how much you need to have saved, you need to know what it is going to cost to live in retirement, compare that to your retirement income, and come up with the amount that investments have to cover.

What I'll often do first is to figure out what the investments can support. The reason I do this first is that if you know what your need is it is likely you'll talk yourself into thinking that your investments can cover it.

In our practice, we use a 4% draw rate as our target. A draw rate is the percentage of the starting value of your retirement portfolio that you'll start drawing out. So if I assume that 4% is doable, if you have $1 million in your investment pool, then you could start your first year by taking out $40,000, which is 4%.

Here's why we like the 4% rule:

REAL-WORLD ACCURATE

First, it is based on actual historical numbers. Why is this important? Because if you assume that you'll get average stock returns and average bond returns and average inflation rates, you will come up with a set of numbers that might make it look like you'll make it through retirement with no money problems at all. But then if the 1930s happen or the 1970s happen or the 2000s happen, then you will run out of money.

If instead we pretended that you retired in 1929, went through a couple of very nasty stock market crashes and the cost of living changes that occurred at the same time, that gives us a better idea of how your portfolio would make it through a crisis.

If we pretended that you retired in 1969, the stock market suffered two major drops over the next 10 years, though not as bad as the Great Depression. But then toward the end of that decade while stocks were recovering, you were hitting a period of hyper inflation. Would your portfolio be able to keep up with these soaring cost-of-living increases?

This 4% rule says yes.

Lasts Though Retirement

Next, it has your portfolio, in those worse-case scenarios, lasting around 30 years. That gets a 65-year-old couple into their mid-90s before the money runs out. And remember, that only happens in a worse case. If the markets aren't bad to you then you'll either be able to increase your spending or leave it as a legacy.

As I alluded to, the draws that you take out of your portfolio are allowed to adjust for inflation. So in our earlier example where you started by taking out $40,000 from your $1 million of investments, if inflation ran 5% that year, the following year you'd be able to take out $42,000 and you wouldn't be hurting your portfolio.

Problems

Now, the 4% rule has its problems (doesn't everything?).

You may need your money to last more than 30 years. In that case in the 1929 or 1969 retirement scenario your money might have run out. There are two ways to cope with this.

The first is to begin by drawing out a smaller amount, say around 3.5%. That draw rate models around 50 years of draws with no problems. Or, you could not increase your draws if the markets don't go up or even lower them if the market drops.

On the other hand, maybe you're retiring later in life or have other moneys to last you the first few years of retirement. In that case the 4% rule is too conservative. You might want a larger draw rate. A 5% beginning value will last around 20 years and give you more money to spend.

Another problem is that this assumes you invest your retirement portfolio in a balanced way. That means you've got about half your money in stocks (40-60%). If you have less than that, while safer in the short-run, your growth will suffer and the portfolio may not be able to keep up with inflation. If you have more, you are susceptible to a dramatic market decline early on to cause you to liquidate too much of your fallen portfolio for enough of it to be around to grow in the future.

Then, it is likely that the inflation adjustment used is probably wrong. The Consumer Price Index does not match a retiree's spending habits. Well, not the average retiree.

And then there are taxes. When I say you can withdraw 4%, I'm talking about a pre-tax number. If your money is in a Roth IRA then your pre- and post-tax number is the same. If it is in a Traditional IRA, then you'll have to pay Uncle Sam first and only get to spend the remainder.

Oh, and the 4% rule, it's not really a rule. It is a guideline based on facts over the last 100 years. Different studies put the number somewhere between 3.5% and 5.0%. But what if the next 100 is very different?

Many professional publications and bloggers are questioning whether the withdrawal rate is set too high. They are worried because, while the historic long-term average on returns of stocks is around 10% per year, most predictions put the next many years at a 5-8% return. And as you can imagine, less return allows less withdrawals. So their logic is based on the idea that if a 4% draw rate is good with stocks returning 10%, you might need to drop things down to 2-3% if stocks are returning less.

While I do not doubt it will be different, I doubt it will be all that much so. After all, last I saw the 30s and the 70s both had some pretty miserable markets, and the 4% rule would have worked then. Are things going to be all that much different? I say no, but I don't know this. I am not a prophet.

Saving For Retirement Takes Discipline

I was reading the other day (see, you're not the only one) and found a report that said only 35% of Americans surveyed by phone thought that a typical middle-income family could save enough for a secure retirement. And that was up from an earlier report that stated less than 30% would be able to save enough. Millennials have even less confidence.

Now I realize that times can be tough; I understand that wages have not kept pace with inflation for years. But

I'm thinking that neither is a good reason for two-thirds of you to think that middle-income America cannot have a secure retirement.

All it takes is discipline.

That's what makes it hard.

It takes discipline to know what it will take to afford retirement. For instance, when someone comes into my office wanting to save for retirement, I'll ask them how much they'll need to live on. They don't know. Fair enough, many feel that's similar to predicting the future, so instead I ask about their current cash flow (or "budget") to give us a starting point. Usually they don't know that either. That's not a problem; after all, that's probably why they are coming to me.

So I have them go home and look at their monthly spending (on recurring bills like electricity), periodic expenses (like vacations), and longer-term savings needs (like the next car). Quite a few don't come back. The assignment is too hard, too boring, or too time-consuming.

It takes discipline to invest for the long-term. The markets go up, the markets go down. People get euphoric, and then they panic (especially if they are going it alone). Part of the reason--they didn't take time to learn about their investments. Did they understand that a short-term loss was not just possible, but likely? Did they prepare themselves for it?

Or did they, like so many others, put long-term money in a short-term investment and short-term money in a long-term investment? Were they so surprised by the gyrations of the markets that they sold at the worst possible time? Most people's savings and investment plans unravel because, frankly, they don't have a plan.

It takes discipline to put the money aside. It takes discipline to put aside rationalization, too. So many times, I've heard that an SUV was not a want but a need; it's just not safe to be out on the road without one. I've also learned that a vacation in the Caribbean is not just a dream, but a family health necessity.

Unfortunately, I rarely hear that putting money away for retirement is essential or a necessity.

Certainly there are families, including middle-income families, who truly cannot save for a secure retirement. My point is those are well below two-thirds of the potential savers out there. The rest who believe that they cannot just don't have the discipline to create and follow a plan.

Here's hoping that you are not among them.

CHAPTER 14
Choosing an Advisor

For some reason, people regularly ask me how to choose a financial advisor. After my stock answer of "choose me," I begin by asking them why they want one. Financial advice means different things to different people.

One such person told me that he had some stocks that he wanted to buy and wanted me to buy them for him. Well, that's not giving financial advice. He did his own research and wasn't interested in other aspects of planning. He didn't want advice; he just needed someone to buy stocks through. For him, calling up (or logging into) a discount broker satisfied his needs.

A recently married woman discussed setting up a trust for her kids and making sure that the money she brought into the marriage made its way to her kids upon her death. She did need some advice, just not financial. She wasn't interested in investments, retirement planning, or any other sort of financial services. I referred her to an estate attorney, the ones who specialize in things like drafting wills and trusts among a host of other estate-related issues.

If you are looking for someone to help with financial planning, investments, and insurance, keep reading. Deciding if you require a financial planner, stockbroker, insurance agent, or CPA for your needs requires some thought. There is no one answer. You may already have trusted professionals you are working with and just need to fill in some gaps. Maybe you're handling the investing yourself, but need someone to help determine if you're saving enough for retirement. You may want a comprehensive plan by a generalist who will act as the quarterback and call in specialists as necessary. Or you may want to choose specialists and act as your own quarterback.

As you can see, before you begin doing homework on the particular professional you'll use, you must understand your goals. Do you, like in my examples, need a place to put the investments you have already researched? Do you need help with your estate? Are you struggling with cash-flow and debt issues? Wondering if you can afford to retire? Want to save some money so your kids can go to college and support you for a change? Did you get a large inheritance or win a jackpot and need guidance on how not to just blow the money? Are you worried about too high a tax bill? Is it life, health, disability, long-term care, and other insurance needs that keep you up at night? The answers to these questions will lead you to the professional(s) you will need.

ADVISOR TYPES

Investment advisor, financial planner, financial advisor, stockbroker, registered investment advisor, insurance agent, retirement planning specialist, personal financial specialist... what the heck do all these mean and what do they all do? Heck if I know. You see, some of the designations above require specific licenses, some infer a certain level of expertise, and some don't have any requirements to them at all.

Instead of going through a very long list, with dozens of possible titles and designations, I'm going to concentrate on those that may have a broader scope of expertise—what you might be looking for if you were asking for a financial planner.

In the world of financial planning there are many designations used, but there are three that I hold in highest regard. The first is the one I carry; I am a Certified Financial Planner™ professional or CFP® professional. The other two that earn my approval and respect: the Personal Financial Specialist (CPA-PFS), and the Chartered Financial Consultant® (ChFC®). Each require formal education, testing, experience in order to be licensed, as well as a commitment to continuing education to stay licensed.

You can find more information on all of these online. The CFP Board website includes the CFP® certification requirements as well as a way to find a Certified Financial Planner™ in your area (www.cfp.net/search/). The American Institute of CPAs (www.aicpa.org) has an overview of the steps CPAs can take to get the Personal Financial Specialist Credential and where to find one. Finally, for information about the Chartered Financial Consultant®, go to www.chfchigheststandard.com.

To me, each has their own "flavor." I find that many Certified Financial Planner practitioners tend to come from a background in the investment field, or from the growing number of college programs specializing in financial planning. The Personal Financial Specialist is actually just part of the title: the full one is Certified Public Accountant-Personal Financial Specialist (CPA-PFS). And as you might suspect, CPA-PFS holders have a certain tax flavor to them. On the other hand, Chartered Financial Consultants® (ChFC®) often come out of the insurance world.

Those flavors don't make one better than another, but do give you some indication of who you might want to shop for first. If you are mainly interested in investing or general financial planning, then maybe the CFP® professional matches you best. Have issues centering more on taxes? Then the CPA-PFS should be on your short-list.

Have general needs, but specific problems in the area of insurance? I'd consider holders of the ChFC®.

That all said, any one of the three can handle most any of your issues, depending on the specific expertise of the advisor. So, just because they may lean toward a certain "flavor," their tastes are influenced by their individual qualifications. Because of this, I wouldn't limit myself to considering just one designation.

WHAT TO DISCUSS WITH YOUR POTENTIAL FINANCIAL ADVISOR

You've found an advisor or three who look like they might be a good fit for you, but how do you know? First, I'd schedule a meeting. Most financial planners and advisors will offer a free introductory meeting so that you can kick their tires and they can see if you're the kind of client they want to work with. Some will charge a nominal fee, but will give advice during the session.

Going into the meeting, the first thing I'd do is to shut up and see what questions the advisor has for you.

"But Gary, if I'm looking for a financial advisor, shouldn't I be the one asking the questions?" Oh, don't worry, you will, but first get a feel for where the advisor is coming from by seeing what they're interested in knowing about you.

You see, some advisors are like the guy whose only tool is a hammer... everything looks like a nail. So if they start explaining how you need a living trust, more life insurance, a particular stock, or that you need to go through some training classes even before they even know anything about you, leave. That's not an advisor, that's a salesman; a pretty poor one, at that.

Now, for your questions. Assuming you've done your homework and know what kind of help you are looking for, ask the potential advisor what experience they have in that area of personal finance. They may sound qualified, but if they have never worked on a case like yours, you don't want to be their guinea pig.

Ask them their qualifications, what it took them to earn those qualifications, and how they maintain their level of expertise. There are many titles and designations that have no requirements other than working long enough at a particular company, or sending in application and a filing fee, sitting through a few hours of a workshop, or passing a very simple test.

Do you want to work with the type of person sitting in front of you? There is no truly wrong answer to this one. Some offices will have a single advisor as your specific point of contact. Others employ a team of people. And some will hand you off to whoever has the specific expertise you need at a particular time. All of these set-ups work—you just need to be aware of it before you hire them.

Ask, "Have you ever been disciplined?" No, we're not worried about the spanking they got when they wrote on the upholstery with crayons, but rather whether any of the professional organizations or regulatory agencies they are licensed under have ever found them less lawful or ethical than you'd like. And don't take their word for it, check it out yourself. The SEC has information and links to direct you to important information about brokers and investment advisors at www.sec.gov/investor/brokers.htm.

Oh, before you leave you probably want to find out what they're going to cost you.

How Financial Advisors Get Paid

You've come to the point where you think you've found a financial advisor who can help you with your problems. Now comes the time you'll want to find out the cost. A simple way to do this? Ask, "What will this cost me?"

There are three typical ways your financial advisor might get paid.

Commission: Depending on what you buy from the advisor or the company, they are paid a percentage of the value of the product sold.

Fee-Only: These advisors are paid either on an hourly basis or they charge a percentage of the investments they're managing for you or a percentage of your net worth. They do not receive commission from any product sales. I'm one of these.

Fee-Based: The advisor charges in the same manner as Fee-Only, but may also make a commission on investment or insurance products you buy. The fee may or may not be reduced based on the commissions received.

So, are commission-compensated advisors biased against their clients' best interests, and the fee-only advisors not? That's a common belief, but as a fee-only advisor, let me assure you that this is not true. While there are a few more issues in the commissioned world, trust me, there are biases in both situations. I'm familiar with many advisors paid on commission who put their customers' interests ahead of profit, and I've seen former fee-only advisors who didn't; they're now sitting in prison for theft and fraud.

In Washington, there's a lot of discussion about something called a fiduciary standard. Some of this has become law but political battles are still being fought over it as I write this so I'm not sure how it will all shake out.

A fiduciary is required to act in the best interest of clients, something the proponents of the standard say should be more important than bigger advisor paychecks. Only a subset of financial advisors were required to act as a fiduciary. The rest were held to a lower suitability standard, where advisors ensure their recommendations are suitable to your situation even if they feel another course of action is better for you. Even under the new law some of the fiduciary protections can be watered down via disclosures given to a client. You might want to read those if that comes up.

Arguments abound in the industry as to whether all financial professionals should adhere to the stricter fiduciary standard. Some believe it would cause the middle class to be effectively ignored by the industry. That's not true. I work under the fiduciary standard and serve dozens of middle-class clients. But let's not argue that now.

Whether an advisor must follow a fiduciary or a suitability standard, you can ask this question: "Regardless of a requirement to act as a fiduciary in regard to me, will you always put my interests above your own?" You see, there are financial professionals who are held only to a suitability standard that nevertheless puts their clients first. Their company may not allow them to put this into writing, but that doesn't stop them from acting in a fiduciary manner.

Personally, I think you should request that they, in action, act as a fiduciary. But that's up to you.

Either way, one last question you need to ask your prospective advisor: "How do you make money from me?"

Be especially observant on how they answer this question. If the advisor gets fidgety, defensive, or sidesteps your question, keep asking. If you hear, "I don't cost a thing," keep prying until you can trace how money makes it from your hands to theirs. Trust me. None of us works for free and the money we earn somehow someway comes from you.

WE'RE HUMAN

One more thing to remember about investment professionals...

I'm going to let you into a little secret. Investment advisors are human. This is true regardless of whether they work for a big-name broker, an insurance agency, or are independent. Each and every one of them is human. And that's a problem.

I've talked about a strange phenomenon among individual (meaning non-professional) investors. They seem to have a bias to get out of the market after it's gone down and a penchant for getting into the market after it's gone up. While they still, on average, make money, they don't make near the money they would have if they had just left their investments in place.

Enter the professionals. You might call them financial planners, financial advisors, investment advisors, or some other such title (I'll answer to just about anything). They do this for a living. You'd think they must be immune to the emotions brought on by a volatile—these days very volatile—market.

You'd think that, but you'd be wrong. You see, it's that human thing. Humans are emotional creatures. It's wired into our brains.

In a Wall Street Journal article, Jason Zweig talked about a study done by TD Ameritrade. They looked at what percentage of cash and bonds was being used by advisors. In October of 2007, which was the high point of the stock market before the financial crisis, advisors had 26% of client assets in bonds or cash. But on March 9, 2009, which was the market low during the credit crisis, those cash and bond holdings had risen to 51%.

Now, there may be some extenuating circumstances. Advisors have to follow their clients' orders, and some clients told their advisors to sell all of the stocks in their portfolios. Also, if they did nothing, the percentage of stocks would have dropped, since the value of stocks plummeted to less than half of their high values during that time period.

But even taking that into consideration, and given my own observations of what many investment professionals did, there was a tendency toward amateurish behavior on their part; many advisors moved to a safer configuration after the markets had gone down.

They got scared.

This isn't to imply that all investment advisors do a poor job of investing; and it doesn't mean that all, or even a majority, of them are not doing a professional job. But it does show that they are human after all, subject to the foibles that plague us all.

"Choose me"

If, after all of that, you're in the market for an advisor I'd be remiss if we didn't share some thoughts on using Personal Money Planning for your investing needs. If you don't want to hear this self-serving message, skip to the next chapter.

One question people ask us: What does Personal Money Planning have that others don't? It's difficult to pinpoint. After all, there are hundreds if not thousands of financial advisory firms in the country that serve their clients well, are honest, build a great investment portfolio, follow the tenets of financial planning, and put their clients first. We are among those.

However I can say when it comes to investing, while we are not the exclusive holders of such, there are three traits that serve us and therefore our clients well:

Emotional Neutrality: I can be opinionated. I can be emotional. I get excited about many topics (ask me about the sport of curling or the game EVE Online sometime). But when it comes to investing I get rather robotic. Maybe it's because I'm an introvert, but the crowds stampeding around affect me little. If my spreadsheet says sell, I sell. If it says buy, I buy. A company that has done great does not impress me. One that does poorly does not disappoint. I may be wrong a lot in the short-term. But that's better than being wrong in the long-term.

Discipline: Even when I get a good "gut" feeling on a client's tolerance for risk, we still run a risk analysis on them. While I may get an idea that an asset class will continue descending into the abyss, if it exceeds our tolerance bands, we begin to build the position back up. While I may want to invest more in an area of the market, if cash flow needs dictate we leave the cash alone, we leave the cash alone. It's our discipline that enforces our emotional neutrality.

Flexibility: Being able to change is critical for long term survival. Success can breed complacency. We continue learning, challenging our notions, asking what could go wrong from here and what could go right. Our target bands have changed over the years. The asset classes we use in our portfolios and their target weights have also changed. Discipline keeps us from doing this in response to current conditions, but rather due to long-term trends. Flexibility can be a great investment virtue, while stubbornness can drastically shorten an investment career.

Still, there are hundreds of firms across the country and thousands of advisors that do the same. So what's different? We love what we do, we're rarely bored, and we have a great sense of humor. But what makes us and everyone else different is how we connect to you.

Come in, sit a spell, ask your questions, and see if you like what we say and how we say it. Can you be free and open with us when it comes to your finances? Does it seem like we can be open with you as well? Do we connect? That's the difference. That's what makes us a good fit or a bad one.

We're certainly not for everyone. But we might be a good match for you.

A PERSONAL NOTE FROM THE AUTHOR
It's Not All About The Money

Investments in and of themselves serve no purpose. Investments are just part of what should be an overall plan to get you where you want to go financially.

We are a financial planning firm. And planning always starts with goals. After all, you need to know where you are going if you are to ever get there. But where do these goals come from? Professed atheist Bertrand Russell stated a very important truth: Unless you assume a God, the question of life's purpose is meaningless.

A few of our clients do not believe in God, and even more are undecided. For those of you who believe in God, start your financial journey there. If not, then you will have to determine your own path in life. Either way, a message in Proverbs is a good place to begin: *He who trusts in his riches will fall, but the righteous will flourish like the green leaf.* (Proverbs 11:28, World English Bible)

Even better is a longer passage from the New Testament. Whether you are a believer or not, I think you'll see the wisdom in it:

But godliness with contentment is great gain. For we brought nothing into this world, and it is certain we can carry nothing out. And having food and raiment let us be therewith content. But they that will be rich fall into temptation and a snare, and into many foolish and hurtful lusts, which drown men in destruction and perdition.

(1 Timothy 6:6-9, King James Bible)

This next part of the same passage is of less significance to those who are not believers, yet I think there's some relevance to all:

For the love of money is the root of all evil: which while some coveted after, they have erred from the faith, and pierced themselves through with many sorrows. But thou, O man of God, flee these things; and follow after

righteousness, godliness, faith, love, patience, meek-
ness.

(1 Timothy 6:10-12)

All of these passages point to the fact that money itself is not a goal. It is not the prize you should seek. To
some it is a gift, and to all it is a tool. We see our job as
one that helps you be the best steward of the money that
you have.

The week before a recent Easter I was thinking about
my faith while at the same time working on client portfolios. "He is risen!" and
"Ensure you have a
non-correlated mix
of growth assets for
retirement!" are not
an obvious mix of
messages. In fact,

> *"It is not the man who has little,*
> *but he who desires more, that is*
> *poor."*
>
> - Seneca the younger, (3BC-65AD)

relative to "He is risen!" the other message really doesn't
matter a whole lot.

That's not to say that if you believe in the resurrection
of Christ that you shouldn't care about your investments.
It does mean that relative to your beliefs your investments
matter very little. And while my beliefs and Easter center
on Christianity, the message works with all religions.

While investments and economics and math and
physics and medicine and engineering are, and must be,
based on science and logic, faith defies that. Though I am

as certain about my faith as I am about the answer to 2 + 2, I freely admit a lack of scientific evidence to prove it. The evidence for faith comes from...well... my faith.

So while some want to make everything of a purely physical realm (such as explaining love as a chemical imbalance in the brain), for the rest of us, there are many things that we consider important which have little basis in human reasoning. A good "for instance" is the idea that God would take the form of man, allow Himself to die as a sacrifice for man, and then come back from the dead and ascend to heaven.

Nope, I've got no good scientific way of proving that one.

Now, this is not a bash against science. I love science, logic, reasoning, education, and even PBS. In fact, I find it a bit appalling when those of faith look down upon such things. Perhaps I'm a bit daft, but I don't really have a hard time reconciling the two.

What I do want to do is to remind people, at least those who have faith in something unseen, to spend some time digging deeper into their faith. Just as I'd like to see folks spend more time working on their retirement planning each year than they do their vacation planning, I'd like to see people who profess a faith to spend more time broadening and deepening their faith than they do working on their investments.

It just seems logical.

For more information about Gary Silverman, CFP® and Personal Money Planning, go to PersonalMoneyPlanning.com.

You can contact Gary by email:
gary@personalmoneyplanning.com
and by phone: 940-692-6885

CPSIA information can be obtained
at www.ICGtesting.com
Printed in the USA
FFOW05n0232281016